# A-Z PRES

C000042631

## CONTENTS

| Map Pages | 2-25 |
| Key to Map Pages | Back Cover |

Index
selecte

## REFERENCE

| | | | | |
|---|---|---|---|---|
| **Motorway** | M55 | **Car Park** (Selected) | P |
| **A Road** | A583 | **Church or Chapel** | † |
| **Proposed** | | **Fire Station** | ■ |
| **B Road** | B6241 | **Hospital** | H |
| **Dual Carriageway** | | **House Numbers** (A & B Roads only) | 246  213 |
| **One-way Street** Traffic flow on A roads is indicated by a heavy line on the drivers' left. | ➡ | **Information Centre** | i |
| | | **National Grid Reference** | 435 |
| **Restricted Access** | | **Police Station** | ▲ |
| **Pedestrianized Road** | | **Post Office** | ★ |
| **Track & Footpath** | | **Toilet** | ▽ |
| **Residential Walkway** | | **with facilities for the disabled** | ♿ |
| **Railway** | Station / Level Crossing | **Educational Establishment** | |
| **Built-up Area** | | **Hospital or Hospice** | |
| **Local Authority Boundary** | | **Industrial Building** | |
| **Postcode Boundary** | | **Leisure or Recreational Facility** | |
| **Map Continuation** | 16 | **Place of Interest** | |
| | | **Public Building** | |
| | | **Shopping Centre or Market** | |
| | | **Other Selected Buildings** | |

## SCALE

1:19000   3.33 inches to 1 mile    5.26cm to 1km    8.47cm to 1 mile

0 — ¼ — ½ — ¾ — 1 Mile

0 — 250 — 500 — 750 — 1000 — 1250 — 1500 Metres

## Copyright of Geographers' A-Z Map Company Limited

Head Office :
Fairfield Road, Borough Green, Sevenoaks, Kent TN15 8PP
Telephone: 01732 781000 (Enquiries & Trade Sales)
       01732 783422 (Retail Sales)
www.a-zmaps.co.uk
Copyright © Geographers' A-Z Map Co. Ltd.

Ordnance Survey® This product includes mapping data licensed from Ordnance Survey® with the permission of the Controller of Her Majesty's Stationery Office.

© Crown Copyright 2000. All rights reserved. Licence number 100017302

Edition 4  2000    Edition 4B  2005 (part revision)

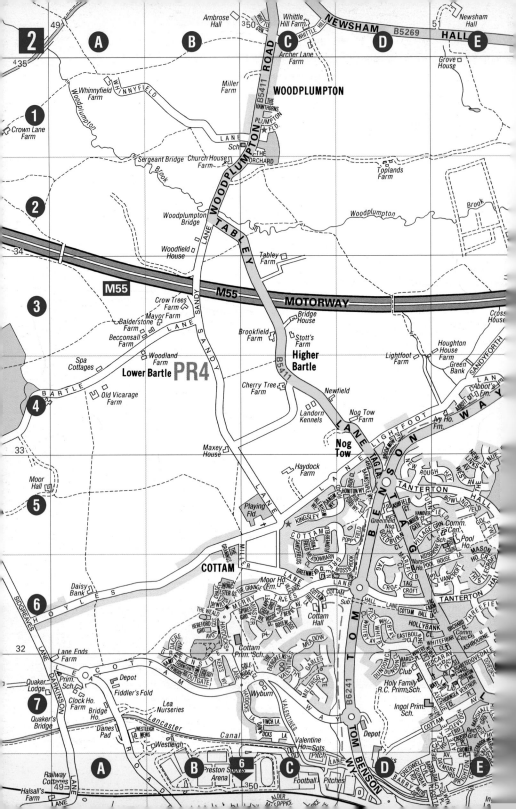

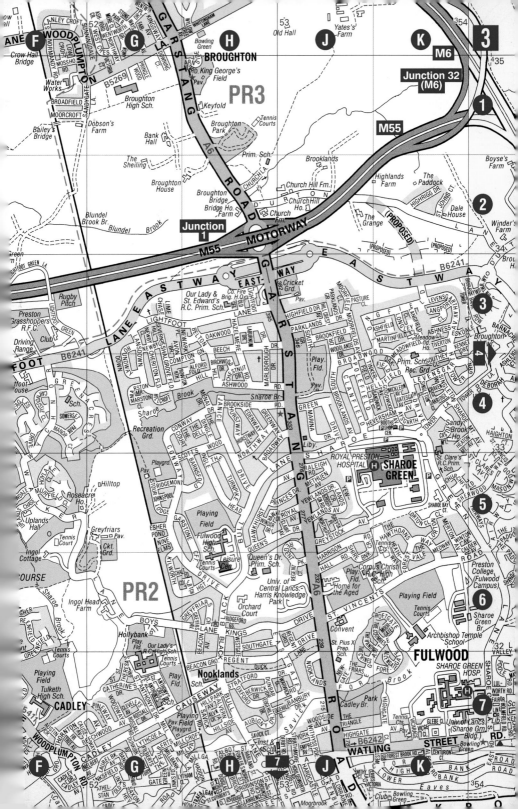

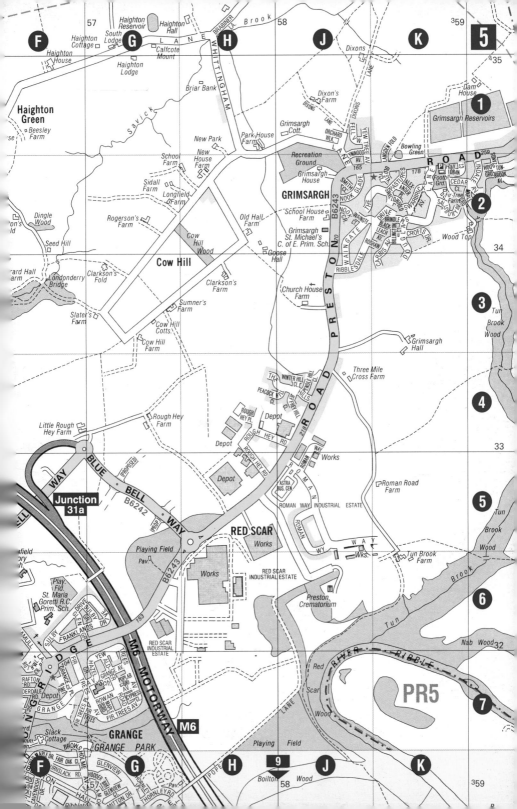

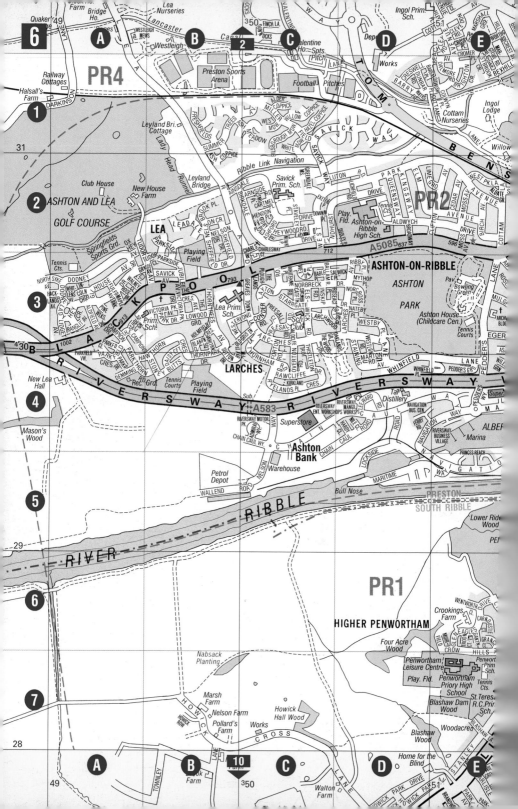

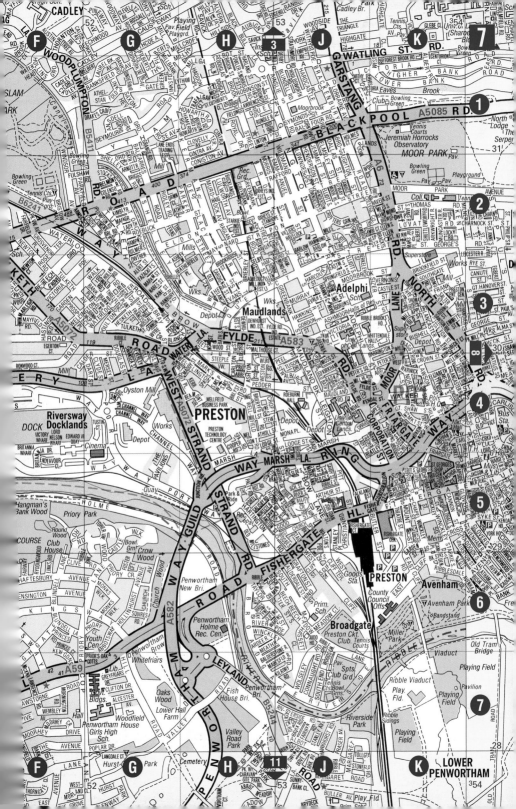

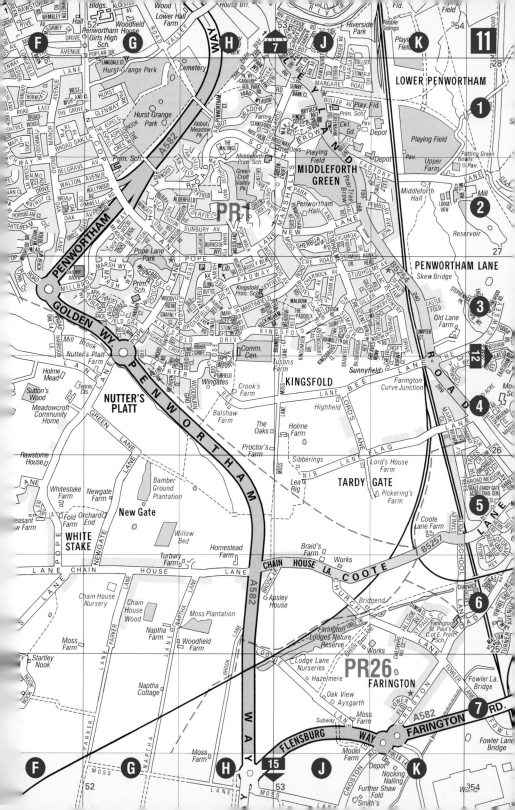

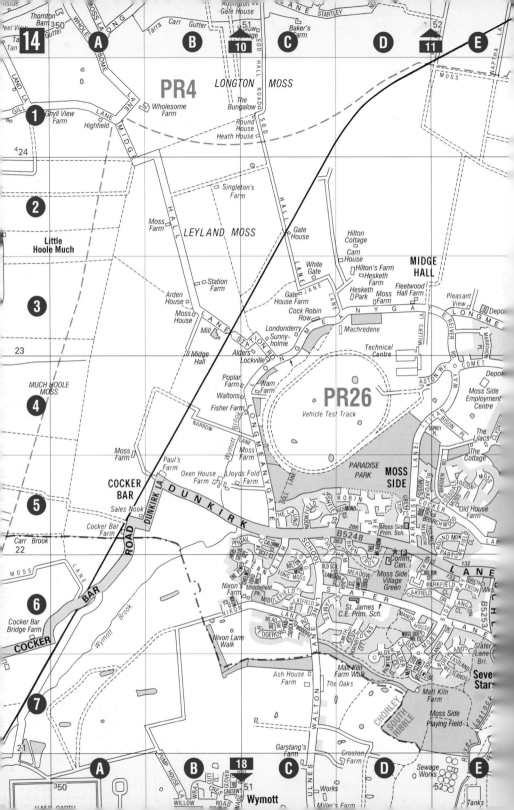

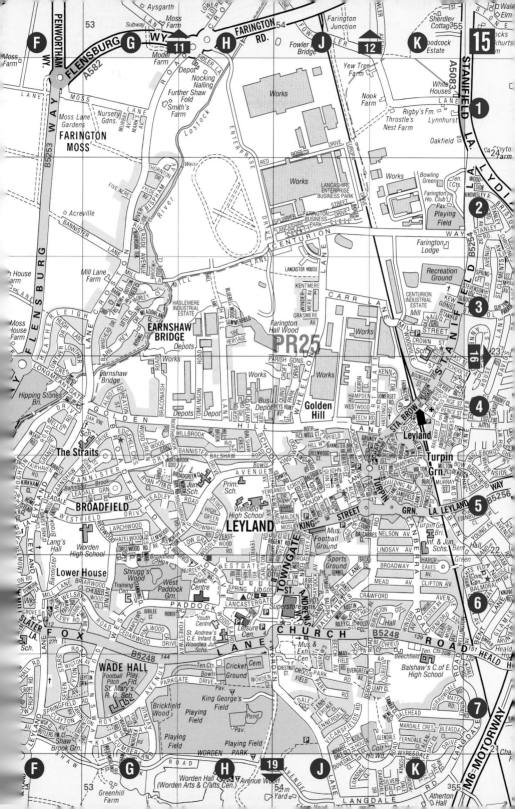

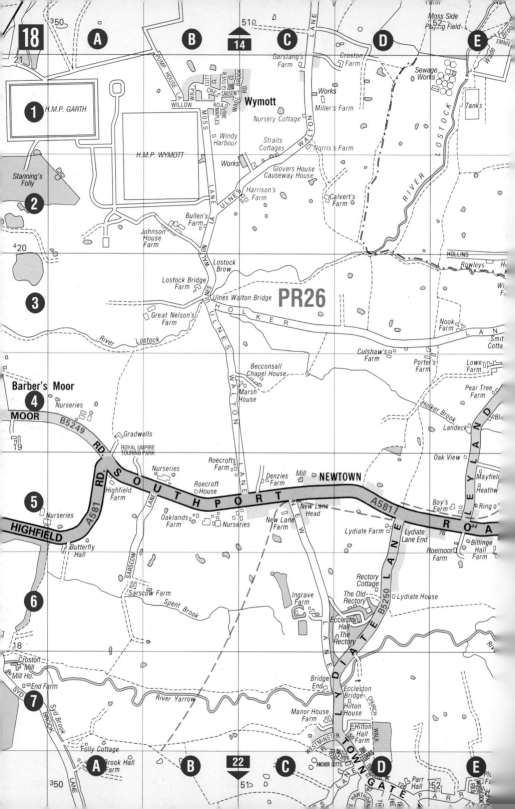

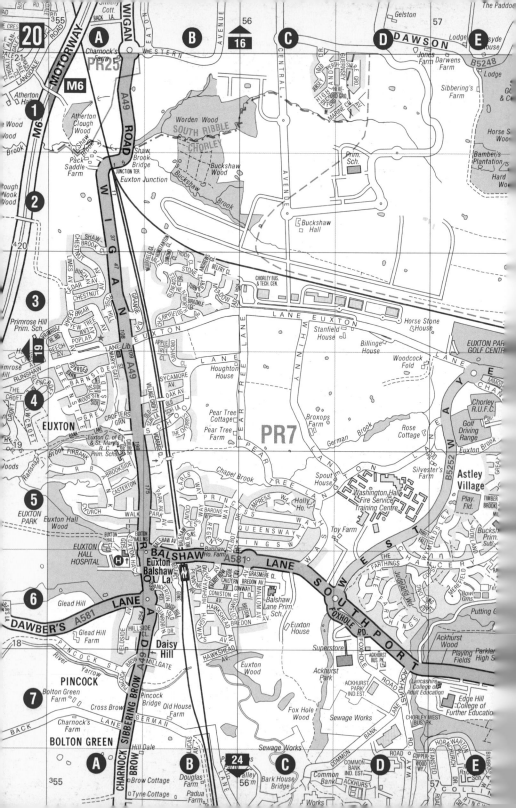

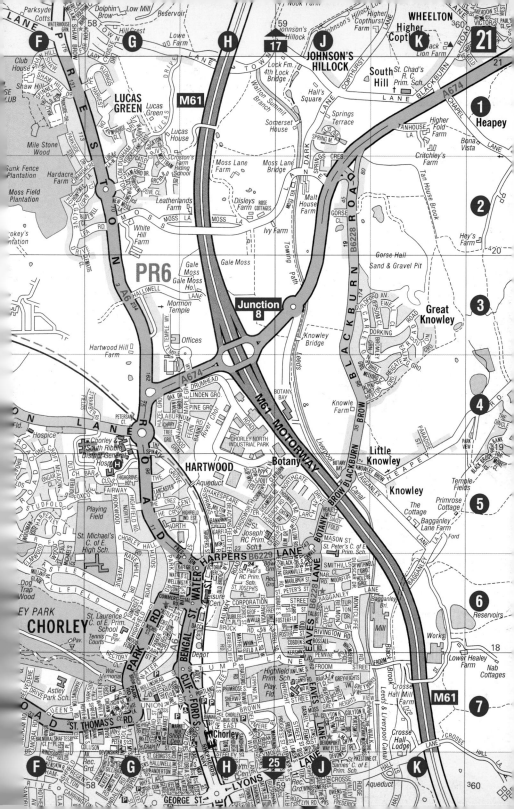

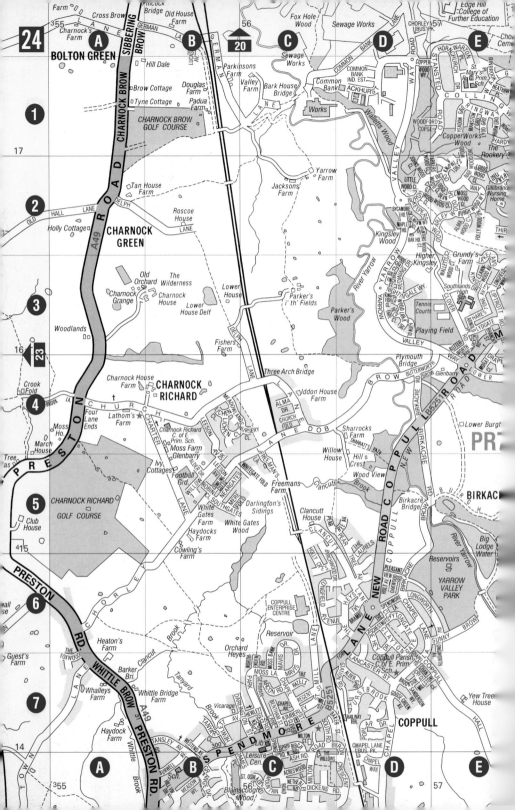

# INDEX

Including Streets, Industrial Estates, Selected Subsidiary Addresses
and Selected Places of Interest.

## HOW TO USE THIS INDEX

1. Each street name is followed by its Posttown or Postal Locality and then by its map reference; e.g. Abbotsway. *Pen* . . . .6G **7** is in the Penwortham Postal Locality and is to be found in square 6G on page **7**. The page number being shown in bold type.
A strict alphabetical order is followed in which Av., Rd., St., etc. (though abbreviated) are read in full and as part of the street name; e.g. Alderfield appears after Alder Dri. but before Alder Gro.

2. Streets and a selection of Subsidiary names not shown on the Maps, appear in the index in *Italics* with the thoroughfare to which it is connected shown in brackets; e.g. *Adelphi Ho. Pres* . . . .3J **7** (off Adelphi St.)

3. An example of a selected place of interest is Ashton & Lea Golf Course . . . .2A 6

## GENERAL ABBREVIATIONS

| | | | |
|---|---|---|---|
| All : Alley | Ct : Court | Lit : Little | Rd : Road |
| App : Approach | Cres : Crescent | Lwr : Lower | Shop : Shopping |
| Arc : Arcade | Cft : Croft | Mc : Mac | S : South |
| Av : Avenue | Dri : Drive | Mnr : Manor | Sq : Square |
| Bk : Back | E : East | Mans : Mansions | Sta : Station |
| Boulevd : Boulevard | Embkmt : Embankment | Mkt : Market | St : Street |
| Bri : Bridge | Est : Estate | Mdw : Meadow | Ter : Terrace |
| B'way : Broadway | Fld : Field | M : Mews | Trad : Trading |
| Bldgs : Buildings | Gdns : Gardens | Mt : Mount | Up : Upper |
| Bus : Business | Gth : Garth | Mus : Museum | Va : Vale |
| Cvn : Caravan | Ga : Gate | N : North | Vw : View |
| Cen : Centre | Gt : Great | Pal : Palace | Vs : Villas |
| Chu : Church | Grn : Green | Pde : Parade | Vis : Visitors |
| Chyd : Churchyard | Gro : Grove | Pk : Park | Wlk : Walk |
| Circ : Circle | Ho : House | Pas : Passage | W : West |
| Cir : Circus | Ind : Industrial | Pl : Place | Yd : Yard |
| Clo : Close | Info : Information | Quad : Quadrant | |
| Comn : Common | Junct : Junction | Res : Residential | |
| Cotts : Cottages | La : Lane | Ri : Rise | |

## POSTTOWN AND POSTAL LOCALITY ABBREVIATIONS

| | | | |
|---|---|---|---|
| *Adl* : Adlington | *Eux* : Euxton | *Ing* : Ingol | *Pen* : Penwortham |
| *Ash R* : Ashton-on-Ribble | *Far* : Farington | *Lea* : Lea | *Pres* : Preston |
| *Bam B* : Bamber Bridge | *Far M* : Farington Moss | *Lea T* : Lea Town | *Rib* : Ribbleton |
| *Bis* : Bispham | *Ful* : Fulwood | *Ley* : Leyland | *Sam* : Samlesbury |
| *Breth* : Bretherton | *Goos* : Goosnargh | *L Grn* : Lightfoot Green | *Stand* : Standish |
| *Brin* : Brindle | *Grims* : Grimsargh | *L Hoo* : Little Hoole | *Walt D* : Walton-le-Dale |
| *Brough* : Broughton | *Haig* : Haighton | *Longt* : Longton | *Wheel* : Wheelton |
| *Char R* : Charnock Richard | *H'pey* : Heapey | *Los H* : Lostock Hall | *Wstke* : Whitestake |
| *Chor* : Chorley | *Hesk* : Heskin | *Lwr B* : Lower Bartle | *W'ham* : Whittingham |
| *Clay W* : Clayton-le-Woods | *High B* : Higher Bartle | *Maw* : Mawdesley | *Whit W* : Whittle-le-Woods |
| *Cop* : Coppull | *High W* : Higher Walton | *Mel B* : Mellor Brook | *Wood* : Woodplumpton |
| *Cot* : Cottam | *Hogh* : Hoghton | *Midg H* : Midge Hall | *Wrigh* : Wrightington |
| *Crost* : Croston | *Hut* : Hutton | *M Side* : Moss Side | |
| *E'ston* : Eccleston | | *New L* : New Longton | |

---

### A

| | | |
|---|---|---|
| Abbey St. *Ash R* . . . . . . . .4H **7** | Albany Dri. *Walt D* . . . . . . .3D **12** | Alexandra St. *Pres* . . . . . . . .5C **8** |
| Abbey Wlk. *Pen* . . . . . . . .3H **11** | Albatross St. *Pres* . . . . . . .2B **8** | Alford Fold. *Ful* . . . . . . . . . .4H **3** |
| Abbot Mdw. *Pen* . . . . . . .1H **11** | Albert Rd. *Ful* . . . . . . . . . . .1K **7** | Alfred's Ct. *Chor* . . . . . . . .1G **25** |
| Abbotsway. *Pen* . . . . . . . . .6G **7** | Albert Rd. *Ley* . . . . . . . . .5A **16** | Alice Av. *Ley* . . . . . . . . . . .5J **15** |
| Abbott Cft. *Ful* . . . . . . . . . .4E **2** | Albert St. *Chor* . . . . . . . .1H **25** | Alice Sq. *Pres* . . . . . . . . . . .3A **8** |
| Abbotts Clo. *Walt D* . . . . .2F **13** | Albert Ter. *High W* . . . . . .1H **13** | Alker La. *Chor* . . . . . . . . .4E **20** |
| Abingdon Dri. *Ash R* . . . . . .3E **6** | Albert Ter. *Pres* . . . . . . . . .3A **8** | Alker St. *Chor* . . . . . . . . .1G **25** |
| Acacia Rd. *Rib* . . . . . . . . . .2E **8** | Albion St. *Chor* . . . . . . . .1G **25** | Allenby Av. *Ful* . . . . . . . . . .7B **4** |
| Acer Gro. *Rib* . . . . . . . . . . .1F **9** | Albrighton Clo. *Los H* . . . . .6B **12** | Allengate. *Ful* . . . . . . . . . . .7K **3** |
| Ackhurst Bus. Pk. *Chor* . . .7D **20** | Albrighton Cres. *Los H* . . . .6B **12** | Allerton Rd. *Walt D* . . . . . .2D **12** |
| Ackhurst Pk. Ind. Est. *Chor* . .7D **20** | Albrighton Rd. *Los H* . . . . .6B **12** | Allington Clo. *Walt D* . . . . .2F **13** |
| Ackhurst Rd. *Chor* . . . . . .7D **20** | Albyn Bank Rd. *Pres* . . . . . .5B **8** | Alma Dri. *Char R* . . . . . . . .4C **24** |
| Acorn Clo. *Ley* . . . . . . . . .6J **15** | Albyn St. E. *Pres* . . . . . . . .5B **8** | Alma Row. *Hogh* . . . . . . . .4K **13** |
| Acorn Clo. *Pen* . . . . . . . . .3F **11** | Alcester Av. *Pen* . . . . . . . . .7G **7** | Alma St. *Pres* . . . . . . . . . . .3A **8** |
| Acrefield. *Bam B* . . . . . . . .1G **17** | Aldate Gro. *Ash R* . . . . . . .2E **6** | Alma Wood Clo. *Chor* . . . .2E **24** |
| Acregate La. *Pres* . . . . . . . .3D **8** | Alder Coppice. *Lea* . . . . . . .1C **6** | Almond Clo. *Ful* . . . . . . . . .5C **4** |
| Acreswood Clo. *Cop* . . . . .7C **24** | Alder Dri. *Char R* . . . . . . . .5B **24** | Almond Clo. *Pen* . . . . . . . .2F **11** |
| Adelaide St. *Pres* . . . . . . . .4B **8** | Alder Dri. *Hogh* . . . . . . . .4K **13** | Almond St. *Pres* . . . . . . . . .4B **8** |
| *Adelphi Ho. Pres* . . . . . . . .3J **7** | Alderfield. *Pen* . . . . . . . . .2H **11** | Alpine Av. *Los H* . . . . . . . .6B **12** |
| (off Adelphi St.) | Alder Gro. *Cop* . . . . . . . . .7D **24** | Alpine Clo. *Los H* . . . . . . . .6B **12** |
| Adelphi Pl. *Pres* . . . . . . . . .4K **7** | Alder Rd. *Rib* . . . . . . . . . . .7G **5** | Alpine Rd. *Chor* . . . . . . . .4J **21** |
| Adelphi St. *Pres* . . . . . . . . .3J **7** | Aldersleigh Cres. *Hogh* . . . .4K **13** | Alsop St. *Pres* . . . . . . . . . . .2K **7** |
| Agnes St. *Pres* . . . . . . . . . .4A **8** | Aldfield Av. *Lea* . . . . . . . . .3A **6** | Alston St. *Pres* . . . . . . . . . .3D **8** |
| Ainscough Brook Ho. *Rib* . . .1F **9** | Aldred St. *Chor* . . . . . . . .1H **25** | Altcar La. *Ley* . . . . . . . . . .2F **19** |
| (off Ribbleton Hall Cres.) | Aldwych Dri. *Ash R* . . . . . . .2D **6** | Alvern Av. *Ful* . . . . . . . . . . .7H **3** |
| Ainsdale Dri. *Ash R* . . . . . . .2B **6** | Aldwych Dri. *Los H* . . . . . .6B **12** | Alvern Cres. *Ful* . . . . . . . . .7H **3** |
| Ainslie Rd. *Ful* . . . . . . . . . .1H **7** | Alert St. *Ash R* . . . . . . . . . .3G **7** | Ambergate. *Ing* . . . . . . . . . .5D **2** |
| Alandale Clo. *Ley* . . . . . . .7K **15** | Alexandra Pavilions. *Pres* . . .3A **8** | Ambledene. *Bam B* . . . . . .7G **13** |
| *Albany Ct. Chor* . . . . . . . .7J **21** | Alexandra Rd. *Walt D* . . . . .2D **12** | Ambleside Clo. *Walt D* . . . .3E **12** |
| (off Devonport Way) | | Ambleside Rd. *Rib* . . . . . . .6E **4** |
| | | Ambleside Wlk. *Rib* . . . . . . .6E **4** |
| | | Ambleway. *Walt D* . . . . . . .1D **12** |

| | |
|---|---|
| Ambrose St. *Ley* . . . . . . . .4K **15** | |
| Amersham Clo. *New L* . . . . .5D **10** | |
| Ampleforth Dri. *Los H* . . . . .4A **12** | |
| Anchor Cotts. *E'ston* . . . . .1C **22** | |
| Anchor Ct. *Pres* . . . . . . . . .5K **7** | |
| Anchor Dri. *Hut* . . . . . . . . .3B **10** | |
| Anderton Rd. *Eux* . . . . . . .6B **20** | |
| Anderton St. *Chor* . . . . . .1G **25** | |
| Andertons Way. *Ful* . . . . . . .6C **4** | |
| Andrew St. *Pres* . . . . . . . . .3C **8** | |
| Aniline St. *Chor* . . . . . . . .7J **21** | |
| Annis St. *Pres* . . . . . . . . . . .4C **8** | |
| Ansdell Gro. *Ash R* . . . . . . .1G **7** | |
| Ansdell St. *Pres* . . . . . . . . .3C **8** | |
| Appleby Clo. *Hogh* . . . . . .4K **13** | |
| Appleby St. *Pres* . . . . . . . . .3K **7** | |
| Applefields. *Ley* . . . . . . . . .7K **15** | |
| Apple Tree Clo. *Eux* . . . . . .3B **20** | |
| Appletree Clo. *Pen* . . . . . . .3G **11** | |
| Aqueduct Mill Ind. Est. *Pres* . .3H **7** | |
| Aqueduct St. *Pres* . . . . . . . .3H **7** | |
| Aqueduct St. Ind. Est. *Pres* . . .3J **7** | |
| Archibald All. *Pres* . . . . . . . .4K **7** | |
| Archway Bldgs. *Ash R* . . . . . .3E **6** | |
| Arcon Rd. *Cop* . . . . . . . . .7C **24** | |
| Ardee Rd. *Pres* . . . . . . . . . .6H **7** | |
| Argyle Rd. *Ley* . . . . . . . . .6J **15** | |
| Argyll Rd. *Pres* . . . . . . . . . .3A **8** | |
| Arkwright Rd. *Pres* . . . . . . .2K **7** | |
| Arley St. *Chor* . . . . . . . . . .7H **21** | |
| Arley Wood Dri. *Chor* . . . . .2E **24** | |
| Armaside Rd. *Cot* . . . . . . . .7B **2** | |
| Armstrong St. *Ash R* . . . . . .2F **7** | |

Arnhem Rd. *Pres* . . . . . . . . . .4D **8**
    (in two parts)
Arnold Clo. *Rib* . . . . . . . . . . . . .2E **8**
Arnold Pl. *Chor* . . . . . . . . . . . .3E **24**
Arno St. *Pres* . . . . . . . . . . . . . .5B **8**
Arnott Rd. *Ash R* . . . . . . . . . . .2G **7**
Arnside Rd. *Ash R* . . . . . . . . . .2C **6**
Arnside Rd. *Brough* . . . . . . . . .1H **3**
Arroyo Way. *Fult* . . . . . . . . . . . .7B **4**
Arthur St. *Chor* . . . . . . . . . . . .1H **25**
Arthur St. *Pres* . . . . . . . . . . . . .5J **7**
Arundel Pl. *Pres* . . . . . . . . . . . .5A **8**
Arundel Way. *Ley* . . . . . . . . . . .6A **16**
Ashbourne Cres. *Ing* . . . . . . . . .6E **2**
Ashby St. *Chor* . . . . . . . . . . . .2G **25**
Ash Coppice. *Lea* . . . . . . . . . . .2B **6**
Ashdown Dri. *Clay W* . . . . . . . .3G **17**
Ashdown M. *Ful* . . . . . . . . . . . .5E **4**
Asheldon St. *Pres* . . . . . . . . . . .3D **8**
Ashfield. *Clay W* . . . . . . . . . . . .3G **17**
Ashfield. *Ful* . . . . . . . . . . . . . . .3K **3**
Ashfield Ct. *Ing* . . . . . . . . . . . . .5D **2**
Ashfield Rd. *Chor* . . . . . . . . . .1F **25**
Ashfields. *Ley* . . . . . . . . . . . . . .5C **14**
Ashford Cres. *Brough* . . . . . . . .1G **3**
Ashford Rd. *Ash R* . . . . . . . . . .2C **6**
Ash Gro. *Bam B* . . . . . . . . . . . .4F **13**
Ash Gro. *Chor* . . . . . . . . . . . . .3G **25**
Ash Gro. *New L* . . . . . . . . . . . .7D **10**
Ash Gro. *Pres* . . . . . . . . . . . . . .3E **8**
Ash Holme. *Pres* . . . . . . . . . . . .1C **8**
Ashleigh Ct. *Ful* . . . . . . . . . . . . .4A **4**
Ashleigh St. *Pres* . . . . . . . . . . .5C **8**
Ashley M. *Ash R* . . . . . . . . . . . .3G **7**
Ash Mdw. *Lea* . . . . . . . . . . . . .1B **6**
Ashmoor St. *Pres* . . . . . . . . . . .3J **7**
Ashness Clo. *Ful* . . . . . . . . . . . .3K **3**
Ash Rd. *Cop* . . . . . . . . . . . . . .7C **24**
Ashton & Lea Golf Course. . .2A **6**
Ashton Clo. *Ash R* . . . . . . . . . .3E **6**
Ashtongate. *Ash R* . . . . . . . . . .3C **6**
Ashton St. *Ash R* . . . . . . . . . . .4H **7**
Ashtree Ct. *Ful* . . . . . . . . . . . . .7E **2**
Ashtree Ct. *High W* . . . . . . . . .2J **13**
Ashtree Gro. *Pen* . . . . . . . . . . .1F **11**
Ashurst Rd. *Ley* . . . . . . . . . . . .5B **16**
Ashwood Rd. *Ful* . . . . . . . . . . . .4H **3**
Ashworth Ct. *Pres* . . . . . . . . . . .6B **8**
Ashworth Gro. *Pres* . . . . . . . . .6C **8**
Ashworth La. *Pres* . . . . . . . . . . .6B **8**
Ashworth St. *Bam B* . . . . . . . . .3F **13**
Ashworth St. *Pres* . . . . . . . . . . .5B **8**
Asland Clo. *Bam B* . . . . . . . . . .5F **13**
Aspden St. *Bam B* . . . . . . . . . .4E **12**
Aspels Cres. *Pen* . . . . . . . . . . .1G **11**
Aspels Nook. *Pen* . . . . . . . . . . .1G **11**
Aspels, The. *Pen* . . . . . . . . . . .1G **11**
Aspen Gdns. *Chor* . . . . . . . . . .2F **25**
Aspinall Clo. *Pen* . . . . . . . . . . .3H **11**
Asshawes, The. *Hth C* . . . . . .7K **25**
Assheton Pl. *Rib* . . . . . . . . . . . .7E **4**
**Astley Hall Mus. & Art Gallery.**
. . . . . . . . . . . . . . . . . . . . . . .6E **20**
Astley Rd. *Chor* . . . . . . . . . . . .6F **21**
Astley St. *Chor* . . . . . . . . . . . .6G **21**
Aston Way. *M Side* . . . . . . . . .4D **14**
Astra Bus. Cen. *Rib* . . . . . . . . .5J **5**
Athelstan Fold. *Ful* . . . . . . . . . .1G **7**
Atherton Clo. *Ash R* . . . . . . . . .2G **7**
Atherton Rd. *Ley* . . . . . . . . . . .6F **15**
Athol Gro. *Chor* . . . . . . . . . . . .2J **25**
Atholl St. *Pres* . . . . . . . . . . . . . .4H **7**
Aubigny Dri. *Ful* . . . . . . . . . . . .7H **3**
Aughton Wlk. *Pres* . . . . . . . . . .3K **7**
Austin Clo. *Ley* . . . . . . . . . . . . .6J **15**
Austin Cres. *Ful* . . . . . . . . . . . . .7F **3**
Avalwood Av. *Longt* . . . . . . . . .5A **10**
Avenham Colonnade. *Pres* . . .6A **8**
Avenham Ct. *Pres* . . . . . . . . . . .5A **8**
Avenham La. *Pres* . . . . . . . . . . .6A **8**
Avenham Pl. *Pres* . . . . . . . . . . .6A **8**
Avenham Rd. *Chor* . . . . . . . . .1G **25**
Avenham Rd. *Pres* . . . . . . . . . . .5A **8**
Avenham St. *Pres* . . . . . . . . . . .5A **8**
Avenham Ter. *Pres* . . . . . . . . . . .6A **8**
Avenham Wlk. *Pres* . . . . . . . . .6A **8**
Avenue, The. *Adl* . . . . . . . . . . .7K **25**
Avenue, The. *Ing* . . . . . . . . . . . .5E **2**
Avenue, The. *Lea* . . . . . . . . . . .3B **6**
Avenue, The. *Ley* . . . . . . . . . . .1H **19**
Avenue, The. *Pen* . . . . . . . . . . . .7F **7**
Avocet Ct. *Ley* . . . . . . . . . . . . .5C **14**

Avon Bri. *Ful* . . . . . . . . . . . . . . .3G **3**
Avondale Dri. *Los H* . . . . . . . . .5B **12**
Avondale Rd. *Chor* . . . . . . . . .1G **25**
Avon Gdns. *Cot* . . . . . . . . . . . .6B **2**
Avon Ho. *Pres* . . . . . . . . . . . . .4D **8**
Aysgarth Av. *Ful* . . . . . . . . . . . .4K **3**
Azalea Clo. *Ful* . . . . . . . . . . . . .5C **4**
Azalea Clo. *Ley* . . . . . . . . . . . .4C **16**

**B**

Bk. Ashby St. *Chor* . . . . . . . . .2H **25**
Bk. Fazakerley St. *Chor* . . . . . .7G **21**
Bk. Grimshaw St. *Pres* . . . . . . . .5A **8**
Back La. *Char R* . . . . . . . . . . . .2H **23**
Back La. *Clay W* . . . . . . . . . . . .4D **16**
    (in two parts)
Back La. *Ley* . . . . . . . . . . . . . . .7A **16**
Back La. E. *Maw* . . . . . . . . . . . .7A **22**
Back La. E. *Maw* . . . . . . . . . . . .7A **22**
Back Mt. *Chor* . . . . . . . . . . . . .7G **21**
Bk. Seed St. *Pres* . . . . . . . . . . .4K **7**
Bk. Starkie St. *Pres* . . . . . . . . . .6K **7**
Badger Rd. *Ley* . . . . . . . . . . . . .2J **15**
Badgers Cft. *Rib* . . . . . . . . . . . .2F **9**
Badgers Wlk. *Eux* . . . . . . . . . . .4F **21**
Badgers Way. *Los H* . . . . . . . . .2B **12**
Bagganley La. *Chor* . . . . . . . . . .5J **21**
    (in two parts)
Bagnold Rd. *Pres* . . . . . . . . . . . .3D **8**
Bairstow St. *Pres* . . . . . . . . . . . .5K **7**
Baker St. *Cop* . . . . . . . . . . . . . .7C **24**
Baker St. *Ley* . . . . . . . . . . . . . .4K **15**
Balcarres Clo. *Ley* . . . . . . . . . . .5J **15**
Balcarres Pl. *Ley* . . . . . . . . . . . .6J **15**
Balcarres Rd. *Ash R* . . . . . . . . . .1G **7**
Balcarres Rd. *Chor* . . . . . . . . . .3F **25**
Balcarres Rd. *Ley* . . . . . . . . . . .6J **15**
Balderstone Rd. *Pres* . . . . . . . . .7H **7**
Baldwin St. *Bam B* . . . . . . . . . .4E **12**
Balfour Ct. *Ley* . . . . . . . . . . . . .5J **15**
Balfour Rd. *Ful* . . . . . . . . . . . . . .1J **7**
Balfour St. *Ley* . . . . . . . . . . . . .5J **15**
Ballam Rd. *Ash R* . . . . . . . . . . . .3C **6**
Balmoral Av. *Ley* . . . . . . . . . . . .6A **16**
Balmoral Ct. *Chor* . . . . . . . . . . .7F **21**
Balmoral Rd. *Chor* . . . . . . . . . .7F **21**
Balmoral Rd. *E'ston* . . . . . . . . .1E **22**
Balmoral Rd. *New L* . . . . . . . . .4E **10**
Balmoral Rd. *Walt D* . . . . . . . . .2D **12**
Balniel Clo. *Chor* . . . . . . . . . . . .1F **25**
Balshaw Av. *Eux* . . . . . . . . . . . .5B **20**
Balshaw Cres. *Ley* . . . . . . . . . . .4H **15**
Balshaw Ho. Gdns. *Eux* . . . . . .5B **20**
Balshaw La. *Eux* . . . . . . . . . . . .6B **20**
Balshaw Rd. *Ley* . . . . . . . . . . . .5H **15**
Balshaw St. *Bam B* . . . . . . . . . .3E **12**
Bamber Bri. By-Pass.
    *Bam B* . . . . . . . . . . . . . . .6E **12**
Bamber St. *Chor* . . . . . . . . . . . .3F **25**
Bambers Yd. *Pres* . . . . . . . . . . .5K **7**
Bampton Dri. *Cot* . . . . . . . . . . . .7B **2**
Banastre. *Chor* . . . . . . . . . . . . .5E **20**
Banbury Dri. *Ful* . . . . . . . . . . . . .7J **3**
Bank Head La.
    *Bam B & Hogh* . . . . . . .5J **13**
Bank La. *Eux* . . . . . . . . . . . . . .4A **20**
Bank Pde. *Pen* . . . . . . . . . . . . .2H **11**
Bank Pde. *Pres* . . . . . . . . . . . . . .6A **8**
Bank Pl. *Ash R* . . . . . . . . . . . . . .3G **7**
Banksfield Pl. *Bam B* . . . . . . . . .6G **13**
Bankside. *Clay W* . . . . . . . . . . . .5F **17**
Banks Rd. *Ful* . . . . . . . . . . . . . . .1G **7**
Bank St. *Chor* . . . . . . . . . . . . . .7G **21**
Bank Top Rd. *Pen* . . . . . . . . . . .2F **11**
Banner Clo. *E'ston* . . . . . . . . . .1D **22**
Bannerman Ter. *Chor* . . . . . . . .5H **21**
Bannister Brook Ho. *Ley* . . . . . .4J **15**
Bannister Clo. *High W* . . . . . . .1H **13**
Bannister Dri. *Ley* . . . . . . . . . . .5F **15**
Bannister Grn. *Hesk* . . . . . . . . .6D **22**
Bannister Hall Cres.
    *High W* . . . . . . . . . . . . . .1H **13**
Bannister Hall Dri. *High W* . . . .1H **13**
Bannister Hall La. *High W* . . . . .1H **13**
Bannister Hall Works.
    *High W* . . . . . . . . . . . . . .1J **13**
Bannister La. *E'ston* . . . . . . . . . .3E **22**
Bannister La. *Far M* . . . . . . . . . .2F **15**
Bannisters Bit. *Pen* . . . . . . . . . .3G **11**

Bannister St. *Chor* . . . . . . . . . .1G **25**
Bar Club St. *Bam B* . . . . . . . . .6E **12**
Barden Pl. *Rib* . . . . . . . . . . . . . .7D **4**
Bardsea Pl. *Ing* . . . . . . . . . . . . .1D **6**
Barleyfield. *Bam B* . . . . . . . . . .3G **17**
Barlow St. *Pres* . . . . . . . . . . . . .2J **7**
    (Brook St., in two parts)
Barlow St. *Pres* . . . . . . . . . . . . .2K **7**
    (Garstang Rd.)
Barmskin La. *Hesk* . . . . . . . . . .7D **22**
Barnacre Clo. *Ful* . . . . . . . . . . . .3A **4**
Barn Cft. *Ley* . . . . . . . . . . . . . . .5D **14**
Barn Cft. *Pen* . . . . . . . . . . . . . . .7F **7**
Barnfield. *Los H* . . . . . . . . . . . .5A **12**
Barn Flatt Clo. *High W* . . . . . . .1G **13**
Barn Hey Dri. *Far M* . . . . . . . . .3G **15**
Barn Mdw. *Bam B* . . . . . . . . . .7H **13**
Barnside. *Ful* . . . . . . . . . . . . . . .5H **3**
Barnside. *Ful* . . . . . . . . . . . . . .4A **20**
Barnstaple Way. *Cot* . . . . . . . . .5D **2**
Barn Vw. *Hth C* . . . . . . . . . . . .7K **25**
Barons Way. *Eux* . . . . . . . . . . .5B **20**
Barra Av. *Ing* . . . . . . . . . . . . . . .1D **6**
Bartle La. *Lwr B* . . . . . . . . . . . . .4A **2**
Bartle Pl. *Ash R* . . . . . . . . . . . . .3C **6**
Bashall Gro. *Far* . . . . . . . . . . . .3K **15**
Basil St. *Pres* . . . . . . . . . . . . . . .2C **8**
Bath St. *Ash R* . . . . . . . . . . . . . .3H **7**
Baxendale Gro. *Bam B* . . . . . . .4E **12**
Bay Rd. *Rib* . . . . . . . . . . . . . . . .2E **8**
Baytree Clo. *Los H* . . . . . . . . . .5C **12**
Bay Tree Farm. *Lea* . . . . . . . . . .4B **6**
Bay Tree Rd. *Clay W* . . . . . . . . .3F **17**
Beacon Av. *Ful* . . . . . . . . . . . . . .6H **3**
Beacon Gro. *Ful* . . . . . . . . . . . .7H **3**
Beaconsfield Av. *Pres* . . . . . . . . .3F **9**
Beaconsfield Ter. *Chor* . . . . . . .5H **21**
Beacon St. *Chor* . . . . . . . . . . .1H **25**
Beamont Dri. *Pres* . . . . . . . . . . .4H **7**
Bearswood Cft. *Clay W* . . . . . . .4F **17**
Beatty Av. *Chor* . . . . . . . . . . . .2F **25**
Beaumaris Rd. *Ley* . . . . . . . . . .6A **16**
Beckett Ct. *Pres* . . . . . . . . . . . . .3K **7**
Bedford Rd. *Ful* . . . . . . . . . . . . .7A **4**
Bedford St. *Chor* . . . . . . . . . . .2G **25**
Beech Av. *Eux* . . . . . . . . . . . . .3A **20**
Beech Av. *Ley* . . . . . . . . . . . . . .6J **15**
Beeches, The. *Brin* . . . . . . . . . .3G **17**
Beechfield Ct. *Ley* . . . . . . . . . .6K **15**
Beechfield Rd. *Ley* . . . . . . . . . .7J **15**
Beechfields. *E'ston* . . . . . . . . . .2D **22**
Beech Gdns. *Clay W* . . . . . . . . .5F **17**
Beech Gro. *Ash R* . . . . . . . . . . .3F **7**
Beechhill Clo. *Walt D* . . . . . . . .2E **12**
Beech Rd. *Ley* . . . . . . . . . . . . . .4J **15**
Beech St. *Pres* . . . . . . . . . . . . . .6H **7**
Beech St. S. *Pres* . . . . . . . . . . . .6J **7**
Beech Ter. *Pres* . . . . . . . . . . . . .6J **7**
Beechway. *Ful* . . . . . . . . . . . . . .7A **4**
Beechway. *Pen* . . . . . . . . . . . . .1F **11**
Beechwood Av. *Ful* . . . . . . . . . .7G **3**
Beechwood Av. *Walt D* . . . . . . .1C **12**
Beechwood Cft. *Clay W* . . . . . .3E **16**
Beechwood Rd. *Chor* . . . . . . . .2J **25**
Bee La. *Pen* . . . . . . . . . . . . . . . .4H **11**
Beenland St. *Pres* . . . . . . . . . . . .3D **8**
Belfry Clo. *Eux* . . . . . . . . . . . . .3B **20**
Belgrave Av. *Pen* . . . . . . . . . . .2F **11**
Belgrave Rd. *Ley* . . . . . . . . . . .6H **15**
Belle Fld. Clo. *Pen* . . . . . . . . . .3A **12**
Bellflower Clo. *Ley* . . . . . . . . . .3C **16**
Bellis Way. *Walt D* . . . . . . . . . .3B **12**
Belmont Av. *Rib* . . . . . . . . . . . . .1D **8**
Belmont Clo. *Rib* . . . . . . . . . . . .2D **8**
Belmont Cres. *Rib* . . . . . . . . . . .2D **8**
Belmont Dri. *Chor* . . . . . . . . . . .6J **21**
Belmont Rd. *Ash R* . . . . . . . . . .2G **7**
Belmont Rd. *Ley* . . . . . . . . . . . .5F **15**
Belton Hill. *Ful* . . . . . . . . . . . . . .3H **3**
Belvedere Dri. *Chor* . . . . . . . . .7F **21**
Belvedere Rd. *Ley* . . . . . . . . . .4K **15**
Bence Rd. *Pres* . . . . . . . . . . . . .5B **8**
Bengal St. *Chor* . . . . . . . . . . . .7H **21**
Bentham St. *Cop* . . . . . . . . . . .7C **24**
Bent La. *Ley* . . . . . . . . . . . . . . .5K **15**
Bentley La. *Bis & Hesk* . . . . . . .7B **22**
Benton Rd. *Rib* . . . . . . . . . . . . .7D **4**
Berkeley Clo. *Chor* . . . . . . . . . .3H **25**
Berkeley Dri. *Bam B* . . . . . . . . .2C **16**
Berkeley St. *Pres* . . . . . . . . . . . .3J **7**

Berry Fld. *Pen* . . . . . . . . . . . . . .2G **11**
Berry St. *Los H* . . . . . . . . . . . . .5A **12**
Berry St. *Pres* . . . . . . . . . . . . . . .5A **8**
Berwick Dri. *Ful* . . . . . . . . . . . . .7H **3**
Berwick Rd. *Pres* . . . . . . . . . . . .6A **8**
Berwick St. *Pres* . . . . . . . . . . . . .3E **8**
Beverley Clo. *Ash R* . . . . . . . . .3G **7**
Bexhill Rd. *Ing* . . . . . . . . . . . . . .1E **6**
Bideford Way. *Cot* . . . . . . . . . . .5D **2**
Bidston St. *Pres* . . . . . . . . . . . . .4E **8**
Billington Ct. *Grims* . . . . . . . . . .2K **5**
Bilsborough Hey. *Pen* . . . . . . . .4J **11**
Bilsborough Mdw. *Lea* . . . . . . . .1C **6**
Binbrook Pl. *Chor* . . . . . . . . . . .1E **24**
Bingley Clo. *Clay W* . . . . . . . . .4G **17**
Birchall Lodge. *Rib* . . . . . . . . . . .7F **5**
    (off Grange Av.)
Birch Av. *Ash R* . . . . . . . . . . . . . .2E **6**
Birch Av. *Eux* . . . . . . . . . . . . . .3A **20**
Birch Av. *Ley* . . . . . . . . . . . . . . .3B **16**
Birch Av. *Pen* . . . . . . . . . . . . . . .2E **10**
Birch Cres. *Hogh* . . . . . . . . . . .4K **13**
Birches, The. *Pres* . . . . . . . . . . . .3C **8**
Birch Fld. *Clay W* . . . . . . . . . . . .3F **17**
Birchin La. *Whit W & Brin* . . . .5G **17**
Birchover Clo. *Ing* . . . . . . . . . . .6E **2**
Birch Rd. *Chor* . . . . . . . . . . . . .5H **21**
Birch Rd. *Cop* . . . . . . . . . . . . . .7C **24**
Birchwood. *Ley* . . . . . . . . . . . . .5E **14**
Birchwood Av. *Hut* . . . . . . . . . .4A **10**
Birchwood Dri. *Cop* . . . . . . . . . .6C **24**
Birchwood Dri. *Ful* . . . . . . . . . . .4H **3**
Bird St. *Pres* . . . . . . . . . . . . . . . .6H **7**
Birkacre Brow. *Cop* . . . . . . . . . .6D **24**
Birkacre Rd. *Chor* . . . . . . . . . . .4D **24**
Birkdale Clo. *Eux* . . . . . . . . . . . .3B **20**
Birkdale Dri. *Ash R* . . . . . . . . . . .2B **6**
Birkett Dri. *Rib* . . . . . . . . . . . . . .1G **9**
Birkett Pl. *Rib* . . . . . . . . . . . . . . .1G **9**
Birk St. *Pres* . . . . . . . . . . . . . . . .5J **7**
Birley St. *Pres* . . . . . . . . . . . . . .4K **7**
Birtwistle St. *Los H* . . . . . . . . . .6B **12**
Bishopgate. *Pres* . . . . . . . . . . . .4A **8**
Bishopsway. *Pen* . . . . . . . . . . . .2H **11**
Bison Pl. *Ley* . . . . . . . . . . . . . . .4E **14**
Bispham Av. *Far M* . . . . . . . . . .2G **15**
Bispham St. *Pres* . . . . . . . . . . . .4K **7**
Blackberry Way. *Pen* . . . . . . . . .3G **11**
Black Brook Clo. *H'pey* . . . . . . .5K **21**
Black Bull La. *Ful* . . . . . . . . . . . .6H **3**
Blackburn Brow. *Chor* . . . . . . . .5J **21**
Blackburn Rd.
    *Chor & Whit W* . . . . . . . .4J **21**
    (in three parts)
Blackburn Rd. *High W* . . . . . . .1H **13**
Blackburn St. *Chor* . . . . . . . . . .1J **25**
Blackcroft. *Clay W* . . . . . . . . . . .3F **17**
Black Horse St. *Chor* . . . . . . . .2F **25**
Blackhurst Av. *Hut* . . . . . . . . . .3C **10**
Blackleach Av. *Grims* . . . . . . . . .2K **5**
Blackpool Rd. *Ful & Pres* . . . . .1J **7**
Blackpool Rd. *Lea & Pres* . . . . .3A **6**
Blackstone Rd. *Chor* . . . . . . . . .6J **21**
Blackthorn Clo. *Lea* . . . . . . . . . .3B **6**
Blackthorn Cft. *Clay W* . . . . . . .4E **16**
Blackthorn Dri. *Pen* . . . . . . . . . .2F **11**
Blake Av. *Los H* . . . . . . . . . . . . .6A **12**
Blanche St. *Ash R* . . . . . . . . . . .3G **7**
Blashaw La. *Pen* . . . . . . . . . . . . .7E **6**
Blaydike Moss. *Ley* . . . . . . . . . .5D **14**
Bleachers Dri. *Ley* . . . . . . . . . . .5G **15**
Bleasdale Clo. *Bam B* . . . . . . . .5F **13**
Bleasdale Clo. *Ley* . . . . . . . . . . .7K **15**
Bleasdale St. E. *Pres* . . . . . . . . . .3B **8**
Blelock St. *Pres* . . . . . . . . . . . . .5A **8**
Blenheim Clo. *Los H* . . . . . . . . .5C **12**
Blenheim Way. *Cot* . . . . . . . . . .5C **2**
Bloomfield Ct. *Pres* . . . . . . . . . . .2J **7**
Bloomfield Grange. *Pen* . . . . . .3G **11**
Blossoms, The. *Ful* . . . . . . . . . . .5C **4**
Bluebell Clo. *Whit W* . . . . . . . .2F **21**
Bluebell Pl. *Pres* . . . . . . . . . . . . .4A **8**
Blue Bell Way. *Ful* . . . . . . . . . . .5E **4**
Bluebellwood. *Ley* . . . . . . . . . . .3H **15**
Blue Stone La. *Maw* . . . . . . . . .5A **22**
Blundell La. *Pen* . . . . . . . . . . . . .6F **7**
Blundell Rd. *Ful* . . . . . . . . . . . . .1J **7**
Boarded Barn. *Eux* . . . . . . . . . .4A **20**
Bodmin St. *Pres* . . . . . . . . . . . . .3D **8**
Boegrave Av. *Los H* . . . . . . . . . .5A **12**
Bold St. *Pres* . . . . . . . . . . . . . . .2H **7**
Bolton Cft. *Ley* . . . . . . . . . . . . .6D **14**

Bolton Mdw. Ley . . . . 6C 14
Bolton's Ct. Pres . . . . 5A 8
Bolton St. Chor . . . . 1G 25
Bone Cft. Clay W . . . . 3F 17
Booths Shop. Cen. Ful . . . . 4K 3
Bootle St. Pres . . . . 3C 8
(in two parts)
Borrowdale Rd. Ley . . . . 7K 15
Bostock St. Pres . . . . 5A 8
Botany Bay. Chor . . . . 4J 21
(in two parts)
Botany Brow. Chor . . . . 5J 21
Boulevard. Pres . . . . 7B 8
Boulevard, The. Walt D . . . . 3B 12
Boundary Clo. E'ston . . . . 1D 22
Boundary Clo. New L . . . . 5D 10
Boundary Rd. Ful . . . . 1H 7
Boundary St. Ley . . . . 4K 15
Bournesfield. Hogh . . . . 4K 13
Bouverie St. Pres . . . . 3E 8
Bow Brook Rd. Ley . . . . 5K 15
Bowers, The. Chor . . . . 3H 25
Bowland Av. Chor . . . . 7H 21
Bowland Pl. Rib . . . . 1G 9
Bowland Rd. Rib . . . . 1G 9
Bow La. Ley . . . . 5K 15
Bow La. Pres . . . . 5J 7
Bowlers Clo. Ful . . . . 6C 4
Bowlingfield. Ing . . . . 5E 2
Bowness Rd. Pres . . . . 3G 9
Bowran St. Pres . . . . 4J 7
Bow St. Ley . . . . 4K 15
Boxer Pl. Ley . . . . 3E 14
Boys La. Ful . . . . 6G 3
Brabiner La. Haig & W'ham . . 1H 5
Bracewell Rd. Rib . . . . 6E 4
Brackenbury Clo. Los H . . . . 6A 12
Brackenbury Rd. Ful & Pres . . 1J 7
Brackenbury St. Pres . . . . 2K 7
Bracken Clo. Chor . . . . 7J 21
Braconash Rd. Ley . . . . 4G 15
Braddon St. Pres . . . . 3D 8
Bradkirk La. Bam B . . . . 5H 13
Bradkirk Pl. Bam B . . . . 6G 13
Bradley La. E'ston . . . . 2E 22
Bradshaw La. Maw . . . . 6A 22
Bradshaws Brow. Maw . . . . 7A 22
Braefield Cres. Rib . . . . 2F 9
Braid Clo. Pen . . . . 4H 11
Braintree Av. Pen . . . . 4J 11
Bramble Ct. Pen . . . . 3J 11
Brambles, The. Cop . . . . 6D 24
Brambles, The. Ful . . . . 5D 4
Brampton Dri. Bam B . . . . 4D 12
Brampton St. Ash R . . . . 3G 7
Brancker St. Chor . . . . 3E 24
Brandiforth St. Bam B . . . . 2F 13
Brandwood. Pen . . . . 1E 10
Brant Rd. Pres . . . . 3G 9
Brantwood Dri. Ley . . . . 5K 15
Brayshaw Pl. Rib . . . . 7E 4
Bray St. Ash R . . . . 3G 7
Bredon Av. Eux . . . . 6C 20
(Cotswold Av.)
Bredon Av. Eux . . . . 6B 20
(Hawkshead Av.)
Bredon Clo. Eux . . . . 6C 20
Breeze Mt. Los H . . . . 5C 12
Brennand Clo. Bam B . . . . 5F 13
Bretherton Clo. Ley . . . . 6E 14
Bretherton Ter. Ley . . . . 5K 15
Breworth Fold La. Brin . . . . 3K 17
Brewster St. Pres . . . . 4J 7
Briar Av. Eux . . . . 3A 20
Briar Bank Row. Ful . . . . 3K 3
Briar Gro. Ing . . . . 7E 2
Briars, The. Ful . . . . 5D 4
Briarwood Clo. Ley . . . . 6G 15
Briary Ct. Bam B . . . . 1G 17
Bridge Bank. Walt D . . . . 6C 8
Bridge Clo. Los H . . . . 5A 12
Bridge Ct. Los H . . . . 5A 12
Bridge End. Los H . . . . 5C 12
Bri. Mill Ct. Chor . . . . 2K 25
Bridge Rd. Ash R . . . . 2G 7
Bridge Rd. Los H . . . . 5C 12
Bridge St. Bam B . . . . 6E 12
Bridge St. High W . . . . 2H 13
Bridge St. Wheel . . . . 7K 17
Bridge Ter. Walt D . . . . 6C 8
Bridgeway. Los H . . . . 5C 12
Briercliffe Rd. Chor . . . . 6H 21

Brierfield. New L . . . . 5D 10
Brierley St. Ash R . . . . 3H 7
Brierly Rd. Bam B . . . . 5G 13
Briers, The. E'ston . . . . 2E 22
Briery Clo. Ful . . . . 7C 4
Brieryfield Rd. Pres . . . . 4H 7
Briery Hey. Bam B . . . . 7J 13
Briggs Rd. Ash R . . . . 2G 7
Brighton Cres. Ing . . . . 1E 6
Brighton St. Chor . . . . 7J 21
Brindle Clo. Bam B . . . . 5H 13
Brindle Fold. Bam B . . . . 6J 13
Brindle Heights. Brin . . . . 1K 17
Brindle Pl. Grims . . . . 2K 5
Brindle Rd. Bam B . . . . 3F 13
Brindle Rd. Brin . . . . 7K 13
(in two parts)
Brindle St. Chor . . . . 2G 25
Brindle St. Pres . . . . 4C 8
Bristol Av. Far . . . . 2A 16
Britannia Dri. Ash R . . . . 5F 7
Britannia Wharf. Ash R . . . . 4F 7
British Commercial Vehicle Mus.
. . . . 5J 15
Brixey St. Pres . . . . 6H 7
Brixton Rd. Pres . . . . 5B 8
Broadfield. Brough . . . . 1F 3
Broadfield Dri. Ley . . . . 4G 15
Broadfield Dri. Pen . . . . 3H 11
Broadfields. Chor . . . . 5F 21
Broadfield Wlk. Ley . . . . 5G 15
Broadgate. Pres . . . . 6H 7
Broadgreen Clo. Ley . . . . 5H 15
Broad Mdw. Los H . . . . 5A 12
Broad Oak Grn. Pen . . . . 2F 11
Broad Oak La. Hut . . . . 3F 11
Broad Oak La. Pen . . . . 1F 11
(in two parts)
Broad Sq. Ley . . . . 6J 15
Broad St. Ley . . . . 6J 15
Broadway. Ash R . . . . 2G 7
Broadway. Ful . . . . 5H 3
Broadway. Ley . . . . 6K 15
Broadwood Clo. Pen . . . . 1F 11
Broadwood Dri. Ful . . . . 4J 3
Brockholes Brow. Pres . . . . 3G 9
Brockholes Vw. Pres . . . . 5C 8
Brock Rd. Chor . . . . 6H 21
Bromley Grn. Chor . . . . 3K 21
Bromley St. Pres . . . . 4H 7
Brook Ct. Ash R . . . . 2G 7
(off Dorman Clo.)
Brook Cft. Ing . . . . 7F 3
Brookdale. Hth C . . . . 7K 25
Brookdale. New L . . . . 6E 10
Brookdale Clo. Ley . . . . 1K 19
Brookes, The. Chor . . . . 1J 25
Brookfield Av. Ful . . . . 7C 4
Brookfield Dri. Ful . . . . 3J 3
Brookfield Pl. Bam B . . . . 7G 13
Brookfield St. Pres . . . . 3K 7
Brookhouse St. Ash R . . . . 3H 7
Brooklands Ash R . . . . 3E 6
Brooklands Av. Ful . . . . 4J 3
Brook La. Char R . . . . 4K 23
Brook La. Wstke . . . . 7H 11
(in two parts)
Brookmeadow. High B . . . . 5D 2
Brook Pl. Lea . . . . 2B 6
Brookside. Cop . . . . 7D 24
Brookside. Eux . . . . 5A 20
Brookside Clo. Far M . . . . 3G 15
Brookside Rd. Ful . . . . 4H 3
Brook St. Ful & Pres . . . . 1H 7
Brook St. High W . . . . 2H 13
Brookview. Ful . . . . 6B 4
Broom Clo. Ley . . . . 3C 16
Broomfield Mill St. Pres . . . . 3K 7
Broughton St. Pres . . . . 1J 7
Broughton Tower Way. Ful . . 3A 4
Brow Hey. Bam B . . . . 7H 13
Brownedge Clo. Walt D . . . . 4D 12
Brownedge La. Bam B . . . . 4E 12
Brownedge Rd.
Los H & Bam B . . . . 5A 12
(in two parts)
Brownedge Wlk. Walt D . . . . 4D 12
Brownhill La. Longt . . . . 6B 10
Brownhill Rd. Ley . . . . 5H 15

Browning Cres. Pres . . . . 2D 8
Browning Rd. Pres . . . . 2D 8
Brown La. Bam B . . . . 3G 13
Brownley St. Chor . . . . 1J 25
Brownley St. Clay W . . . . 5F 17
Browns Hey. Chor . . . . 5E 20
Brown St. Bam B . . . . 5F 13
Brown St. Chor . . . . 7H 21
Browsholme Av. Rib . . . . 7F 5
Brunswick Pl. Ash R . . . . 3G 7
Brunswick St. Chor . . . . 7H 21
Brydeck Av. Pen . . . . 1J 11
Buchanan St. Chor . . . . 1H 25
Buckingham Av. Pen . . . . 3H 11
Buckingham St. Chor . . . . 1H 25
Bucklands Av. Ash R . . . . 2H 7
Buckshaw Hall Clo. Chor . . . . 5F 21
Buckton Clo. Whit W . . . . 1G 21
Bude Clo. Cot . . . . 5D 2
Buffalo Rd. Ley . . . . 2J 15
(off Country Clo.)
Buller Av. Pen . . . . 1J 11
Bullfinch St. Pres . . . . 3B 8
Bulmer St. Ash R . . . . 2G 7
Burgh Hall Rd. Chor . . . . 5E 24
Burgh La. Chor . . . . 4G 25
Burgh La. S. Cop . . . . 6F 25
Burghley Clo. Clay W . . . . 4G 17
Burghley Ct. Ley . . . . 5K 15
Burgh Meadows. Chor . . . . 4G 25
Burgh Wood Way. Chor . . . . 2D 24
Burholme Clo. Rib . . . . 2G 9
Burholme Pl. Rib . . . . 2G 9
Burholme Rd. Rib . . . . 2G 9
Burleigh Rd. Pres . . . . 5H 7
Burlington Gdns. Ley . . . . 6K 15
Burlington St. Chor . . . . 1H 25
Burnsall Pl. Rib . . . . 7E 4
Burnside Av. Rib . . . . 1F 9
Burnside Way. Pen . . . . 2H 11
Burnslack Rd. Rib . . . . 1F 9
Burns St. Pres . . . . 2D 8
Burrington Clo. Ful . . . . 5D 4
Burrow Rd. Pres . . . . 3A 8
Burwell Av. Cop . . . . 7B 24
Burwood Clo. Pen . . . . 4K 11
Burwood Dri. Rib . . . . 1E 8
Bushell Pl. Pres . . . . 6A 8
Bushell St. Pres . . . . 3K 7
Bussel Rd. Pen . . . . 3J 11
Butcher Brow. Walt D . . . . 7E 8
Butler Pl. Pres . . . . 2K 7
Butlers Farm Ct. Ley . . . . 7F 15
Butler St. Pres . . . . 5K 7
Butterlands. Pres . . . . 4F 9
Buttermere Av. Chor . . . . 2E 24
Buttermere Clo. Ful . . . . 7C 4
Buttermere Clo. Walt D . . . . 3D 12
Butterworth Brow. Chor . . . . 4D 24
Bymbrig Clo. Bam B . . . . 5E 12
Byre Vw. Hth C . . . . 7K 25
Byron Cres. Cop . . . . 7C 24
Byron St. Chor . . . . 7G 21

# C

Cadley Av. Ful . . . . 1F 7
Cadley Causeway. Ful . . . . 1G 7
Cadley Dri. Ful . . . . 1F 7
Cadogan Pl. Pres . . . . 6A 8
Cage La. New L . . . . 5F 11
Cairndale Dri. Ley . . . . 1K 19
Cairnsmore Av. Pres . . . . 3F 9
Calder Av. Chor . . . . 3F 25
Calder Av. Ful . . . . 5K 3
Calderbank Clo. Ley . . . . 5C 14
Calder St. Ash R . . . . 4F 7
Callon St. Pres . . . . 4D 8
Calverley St. Pres . . . . 3D 8
Cambridge Clo. Pres . . . . 2J 7
Cambridge Ct. Pres . . . . 2J 7
Cambridge Rd. Bam B . . . . 5F 13
Cambridge St. Chor . . . . 1G 25
Cambridge St. Pres . . . . 2J 7
Cambridge Wlk. Pres . . . . 2J 7
Cam Clo. Bam B . . . . 5F 13
Camden Pl. Pres . . . . 5K 7
Camelot Theme Pk. . . . . 4H 23
Cameron Cft. Chor . . . . 7H 21
Camomile Clo. Chor . . . . 4E 20

Campbell St. Pres . . . . 4B 8
Campion Dri. Lea . . . . 3A 6
Campions, The. Lea . . . . 3A 6
Cam St. Pres . . . . 2C 8
Camwood. Bam B . . . . 2F 17
Camwood Dri. Los H . . . . 4B 12
Cam Wood Fold. Clay W . . . . 3E 16
Canal Wlk. Chor . . . . 7J 21
Canberra Rd. Ley . . . . 5K 15
Cann Bri. St. High W . . . . 1H 13
Cannon Hill. Ash R . . . . 3G 7
Cannon St. Chor . . . . 7G 21
Cannon St. Pres . . . . 5K 7
Canterbury Rd. Pres . . . . 3D 8
Canterbury St. Chor . . . . 2J 25
Cantsfield Av. Ing . . . . 7F 3
Canute St. Pres . . . . 3A 8
Capesthorne Dri. Chor . . . . 5F 25
Capital Way. Walt D . . . . 7C 8
Capitol Cen. Walt D . . . . 7C 8
Carbis Av. Grims . . . . 3K 5
Cardigan St. Ash R . . . . 3H 7
Carleton Av. Ful . . . . 7D 4
Carleton Dri. Pen . . . . 1E 10
Carleton Rd. Chor . . . . 3J 21
Carlisle Av. Pen . . . . 1E 10
Carlisle Ho. Pres . . . . 5A 8
(off Arundel Pl.)
Carlisle Pl. Adl . . . . 7K 25
Carlisle St. Pres . . . . 4A 8
Carloway Av. Ful . . . . 6C 4
Carlton Av. Clay W . . . . 4F 17
Carlton Dri. Pres . . . . 7B 8
Carlton Rd. Ley . . . . 6H 15
Carlton St. Ash R . . . . 4H 7
Carnarvon Rd. Pres . . . . 5H 7
Carnfield Pl. Bam B . . . . 5H 13
Carnoustie Clo. Ful . . . . 4F 3
Carnoustie Ct. Pen . . . . 6E 6
Caroline St. Pres . . . . 3C 8
Carr Barn Brow. Bam B . . . . 7J 13
Carr Brook Clo. Whit W . . . . 6F 17
Cardale. Hut . . . . 3B 10
Carr Fld. Bam B . . . . 2G 17
Carr Ho. La. Wrigh . . . . 7H 23
Carrington Cen., The.
E'ston . . . . 2E 22
Carrington Rd. Chor . . . . 1F 25
Carr La. Chor . . . . 3G 25
Carr La. Far . . . . 3J 15
Carr Mdw. Bam B . . . . 7J 13
Carrol St. Pres . . . . 3B 8
Carr Pl. Bam B . . . . 6H 13
Carr Rd. Clay W . . . . 4F 17
Carr St. Bam B . . . . 5E 12
Carr St. Chor . . . . 6J 21
Carr St. Pres . . . . 5B 8
Carrwood Rd. Walt D . . . . 2A 12
Carrwood Way. Walt D . . . . 2B 12
Carter St. Pres . . . . 5H 7
Cartmel Pl. Ash R . . . . 2C 6
(in two parts)
Cartmel Rd. Ley . . . . 6F 15
Carver Brow. High W . . . . 1K 13
Carwood La. Whit W . . . . 7G 17
(in two parts)
Casterton. Eux . . . . 5A 20
Castle Fold. Pen . . . . 3K 11
Castle Mt. Ful . . . . 4K 3
Castle St. Chor . . . . 1H 25
Castle St. Pres . . . . 3K 7
Castleton Rd. Pres . . . . 3B 8
Castle Wlk. Pen . . . . 5G 7
Catforth Rd. Ash R . . . . 3C 6
Catherine St. Chor . . . . 2G 25
Catherine St. Pres . . . . 4B 8
Cathrow Dri. New L . . . . 6E 10
Catley Clo. Whit W . . . . 2G 21
Caton Dri. Ley . . . . 4C 16
Causeway Av. Ful . . . . 7F 3
Causeway, The. Chor . . . . 7J 21
Causeway, The. Ley . . . . 1B 18
Cavendish Cres. Rib . . . . 1F 9
Cavendish Dri. Rib . . . . 1F 9
Cavendish Pl. Walt D . . . . 2D 12
Cavendish Rd. Pres . . . . 3E 8
Cavendish St. Chor . . . . 1J 25
Cave St. Pres . . . . 4D 8
Cawsey, The. Pen . . . . 3K 11
Caxton Rd. Ful . . . . 3B 4
Cecilia St. Pres . . . . 3D 8
Cedar Av. Ash R . . . . 2E 6

Cedar Av. Eux .............3A 20
Cedar Av. Los H .........5B 12
Cedar Clo. Grims ........2K 5
Cedar Fld. Clay W ........4G 17
Cedar Ho. Chor .........2D 24
(off Hunters Wood Ct.)
Cedar Rd. Chor .........5H 21
Cedar Rd. Rib ..........2E 8
Cedars, The. Chor ......4F 25
Cedars, The. E'ston ....1D 22
Cedars, The. New L .....5D 10
Cedar Way. Pen .........2F 11
Cedarwood Dri. Ley .....6G 15
Cemetery Rd. Pres ......3C 8
Centenary Mill Ct. Pres ..4B 8
Central Av. Eux ........1C 20
Central Av. Hogh .......3K 13
Central Dri. Pen .......1D 10
Centre Dri. Clay W .....2F 17
Centurion Ct. Ful ......1K 7
Centurion Ind. Est. Far ..3K 15
Centurion Way. Far .....2J 15
Chaddock St. Pres ......5K 7
Chadwick Gdns. Los H ....6A 12
Chain Caul Rd. Ash R ....4C 6
Chain Caul Way. Ash R ...4C 6
Chain Ho. La. Wstke ....6F 11
Chalfont Fld. Ful ......6G 3
Chancery Clo. Cop ......7D 24
Chancery Rd. Chor ......4E 20
Chandler Bus. Pk. Ley ....4G 15
(off Talbot Rd.)
Chandler St. Pres ......4J 7
Channel Way. Ash R .....4G 7
Chapel Brow. Ley .......4K 15
Chapel La. Cop .........6D 24
Chapel La. H'pey .......1K 21
Chapel La. Longt .......5A 10
Chapel La. New L .......5B 10
Chapel La. Bus. Pk. Cop ..7D 24
Chapel Mdw. Longt ......5A 10
Chapel Pk. Rd. Longt ...5A 10
Chapel Rd. Ful .........7A 4
Chapel St. Chor ........7G 21
(in two parts)
Chapel St. Cop .........7C 24
Chapel St. Pres ........5K 7
Chapel Wlk. Pres .......5K 7
Chapel Way. Cop ........7D 24
Chapel Yd. Cop .........7D 24
Chapel Yd. Walt D ......7D 8
Chapman Rd. Ful ........1A 8
Charles Cres. Hogh .....2J 13
Charleston Ct. Bam B ...4E 12
Charles Way. Ash R .....2C 6
Charlesway Ct. Lea .....3C 6
Charlotte Pl. Pres .....5A 8
Charlotte St. Pres .....5A 8
Charnley Clo. Pen ......3G 11
Charnley Fold. Walt D ..2F 13
Charnley Fold Ind. Est.
  Bam B ...............2F 13
Charnley Fold La. Bam B ..2F 13
Charnley St. Pres ......5K 7
Charnock Av. Pen .......3J 11
Charnock Brow. Char R ..1A 24
**Charnock Brow Golf Course.**
  ....................1B 21
Charnock Fold. Pres ....2A 8
Charnock Ho. Chor ......5G 21
(off Lancaster Ct.)
**Charnock Richard Golf Course.**
  ....................5A 24
Charnock St. Chor ......1H 25
Charnock St. Ley .......5J 15
Charnock St. Pres ......2A 8
Charter La. Char R .....4B 24
Chartwell Clo. Clay W ..4G 17
Chartwell Ri. Los H ....5C 12
Chasden Clo. Whit W ....2G 21
Chase, The. Cot ........6B 2
Chase, The. Ley ........4A 16
Chatburn Rd. Rib .......7E 4
Chatham Pl. Chor .......7J 21
Chatham Pl. Pres .......2B 8
Chatsworth Clo. Chor ...7F 21
Chatsworth Rd. Hth C ...7K 25
Chatsworth Rd. Ley .....5J 15
Chatsworth Rd. Walt D ..2D 12
Chatsworth St. Pres ....4C 8
Chaucer Clo. E'ston ....2D 22

Chaucer St. Pres .......2D 8
Cheam Av. Chor .........2H 25
Cheapside. Chor ........1G 25
Cheapside. Pres ........5K 7
Cheddar Dri. Ful .......5D 4
Cheetham Mdw. Ley ......5C 14
Chelford Clo. Pen ......4K 11
Chelmsford Gro. Chor ...1F 25
Chelmsford Pl. Chor ....1F 25
Chelmsford Wlk. Ley ....6C 14
Cheriton Fld. Ful ......4G 3
Cherries, The. Eux .....4B 20
Cherry Clo. Ful ........5D 4
Cherryfields. Eux ......3B 20
Cherry Tree Gro. Chor ..4G 21
Cherry Trees. Los H ....2C 12
Cherry Wood. Pen .......2E 10
Cherrywood Clo. Ley ....6G 15
Chesham Dri. New L .....5D 10
Cheshire Ho. Clo. Far M ..6K 11
Chesmere Dri. Pen ......7F 7
Chester Av. Chor .......4J 25
Chester Rd. Pres .......3C 8
Chestnut Av. Chor ......5J 21
Chestnut Av. Eux .......2A 20
Chestnut Av. Pen .......1E 10
Chestnut Clo. Walt D ...3E 12
Chestnut Ct. Ley .......7J 15
Chestnut Cres. Rib .....2E 8
Chestnut Dri. Ful ......4H 3
Chestnuts, The. Cop ....6D 24
Cheviot St. Pres .......4H 7
Chiltern Av. Eux .......6B 20
Chiltern Mdw. Ley ......5B 16
Chindits Way. Ful ......7B 4
Chines, The. Ful .......7J 3
Chingle Clo. Ful .......5E 4
Chisnall La. Hesk ......6H 23
Chorley Bus. & Technology Cen.
  Eux .................3C 20
**Chorley F.C.** ............2G 25
(Victory Pk.)
**Chorley Golf Course.** ...4K 25
Chorley Hall Rd. Chor ..5G 21
Chorley N. Ind. Pk. Chor ..4H 21
Chorley Old Rd.
  Whit W & Brin .......7G 17
Chorley Retail Pk. Chor ..1H 25
Chorley Rd. Hth C ......5K 25
Chorley Rd. Walt D .....1D 12
**Chorley R.U.F.C.** .......4E 20
(Brookfields Chancery Rd.)
**Chorley W. Bus. Pk.** Chor ..7D 20
Christ Chu. St. Pres ...5J 7
Christian Rd. Pres .....5J 7
Church Av. Pen .........6G 7
Church Av. Pres ........4E 8
Church Brow. Chor ......7G 21
Church Brow. Walt D ....7D 8
Church Ct. Pres ........2C 8
Churchfield. Ful .......5K 3
Church Fold. Char R ....4C 24
Church Gdns. Eux .......4A 20
Church Hill. Whit W ....7F 17
Churchill Rd. Ful ......7C 4
Churchill Way. Ley .....4J 15
Church La. Brough ......2H 3
Church La. Char R ......4A 24
Church La. Wstke & Far M ..6J 11
Church M. Bam B ........6E 12
Church Rd. Bam B .......6E 12
(in three parts)
Church Rd. Ley .........6J 15
Church Row. Pres .......4A 8
Churchside. New L ......5D 10
Church St. Chor ........1G 25
Church St. High W ......2H 13
Church St. Ley .........4K 15
Church St. Pres ........5A 8
Church Ter. High W .....2H 13
Church Wlk. E'ston .....7D 18
Church Wlk. Eux ........5A 20
Cinnamon Ct. Pen .......3G 11
Cinnamon Hill Dri. N.
  Walt D ..............2D 12
Cinnamon Hill Dri. S.
  Walt D ..............2D 12
Cintra Av. Ash R .......1H 7
Cintra Ter. Ash R ......1H 7
Clairane Av. Ful .......5J 3
Clancut La. Cop ........5C 24

Clanfield. Ful .........4J 3
Clara St. Pres .........5C 8
Claremont Av. Chor .....1F 25
Claremont Av. Ley ......6K 15
Claremont Rd. Chor .....3F 25
Clarence St. Chor ......1H 25
Clarence St. Ley .......4K 15
Clarence St. Ind. Est.
  Chor ................1H 25
(off Clarence St.)
Clarendon St. Chor .....1J 25
Clarendon St. Pres .....6A 8
Claughton Av. Ley ......5C 16
Clayburn Clo. Chor .....5H 21
Clayton Av. Ley ........7F 15
Clayton Brook Rd. Bam B ..1F 15
Claytongate. Cop .......6D 24
Claytongate Dri. Pen ...3A 12
Clayton Grn. Bus. Pk.
  Clay W ..............2F 17
Clayton Grn. Cen. Clay W ..2F 17
Clayton Grn. Rd. Clay W ..3E 16
Clayton's Ga. Pres .....4K 7
Clayton St. Bam B ......4E 12
Claytonvilla Fold. Clay W ..3E 16
Clematis Clo. Chor .....4E 20
Clevedon Rd. Ing .......7E 2
Cleveland Av. Ful ......7C 4
Cleveland Rd. Ley ......4H 15
Cleveland St. Chor .....7G 21
Cleveland St. Cop ......7C 24
Cleveleys Av. Ful ......7G 3
Cleveleys Rd. Hogh .....2K 13
Cliffe Ct. Pres ........4D 8
Cliffe Dri. Whit W .....6F 17
Clifford St. Chor ......7H 21
Cliff St. Pres .........6J 7
Clifton Av. Ash R ......2D 6
Clifton Av. Ley ........6K 15
Clifton Cres. Pres .....2C 8
Clifton Dri. Pen .......7G 7
Clifton Gro. Chor ......1F 26
Clifton Gro. Pres ......1C 8
Clifton Ho. Ful ........7C 4
Clifton Pde. Far .......3A 16
Clifton Pl. Ash R ......2F 7
Clifton St. Pres .......6H 7
Clitheroe St. Pres .....5C 8
Clive Rd. Pen ..........6F 7
Cloisters, The. Ash R ..4H 7
Cloisters, The. Ley ....4A 16
Close, The. Ful ........5E 4
Close, The. New L ......5D 10
(in two parts)
Close, The. Walt D .....3B 12
Clough Acre. Chor ......5E 20
Clough Av. Walt D ......2B 12
Cloughfield. Pen .......4H 11
Clough, The. Clay W ....3E 16
Clovelly Av. Ash R .....1H 7
Clovelly Dri. Pen ......7E 6
Clover Fld. Clay W .....4F 17
Cloverfield. Pen .......1F 11
Clover Rd. Chor ........3E 24
Club St. Bam B .........6E 12
Clydesdale Pl. Ley .....4E 14
Clyde St. Ash R ........4G 7
Coach Ho., The. Eux ....2H 19
Cobden St. Chor ........6J 21
Cocker Bar Rd. Ley .....6A 14
Cocker La. Ley .........5D 14
Cocker Rd. Bam B .......6G 13
Cockersand Av. Hut .....4A 10
Cold Bath St. Pres .....4J 7
Colebatch. Ful .........6H 3
Colenso Rd. Ash R ......2G 7
Coleridge Clo. Cot .....7C 2
College Ct. Pres .......2J 7
Collingwood Rd. Chor ...1E 24
Collinson St. Pres .....3C 8
Collins Rd. Bam B ......4E 12
Collins Rd. N. Bam B ...3F 13
Collison Av. Chor ......7G 21
Colman Ct. Pres ........6H 7
Colt Ho. Clo. Ley ......7J 15
Coltsfoot Dri. Chor ....5H 21
Columbine Clo. Chor ....4E 20
Colwyn Pl. Ing .........1E 6
Colyton Clo. Chor ......7J 21
Colyton Rd. Chor .......7J 21
Colyton Rd. E. Chor ....7J 21
Comet Rd. M Side .......4E 14

Commercial Rd. Chor ....6G 21
Comn. Bank Ind. Est.
  Chor ................1D 24
Comn. Bank La. Chor ....1D 24
Compton Grn. Ful .......4G 3
Conder Rd. Ash R .......3C 6
Condor Way. Pen ........3A 12
Congress Way. Chor .....6G 21
Coniston Av. Ash R .....2H 7
Coniston Av. Eux .......6B 20
Coniston Dri. Walt D ...3D 12
Coniston Rd. Chor ......2F 25
Coniston Rd. Ful .......6C 4
Connaught Rd. Pres .....7J 7
Constable Av. Los H ....6A 12
Constable St. Pres .....4A 8
Convent Clo. Bam B .....4D 12
Convent Clo. Ley .......4A 16
Conway Av. Pen .........4A 12
Conway Clo. Eux ........6C 20
Conway Ct. Hogh ........3K 13
Conway Dri. Ful ........4G 3
Conway Ho. Pres ........4D 8
Conway Rd. E'ston ......1E 22
Coombes, The. Ful ......6K 3
Co-operative St. Bam B ..5E 12
Cooper Hill Clo. Walt D ..7D 8
Cooper Hill Dri. Walt D ..7D 8
Cooper Rd. Pres ........4H 7
Coopers Fold. Rib ......2G 9
Cooper's La. Hesk ......7D 22
Coote La. Wstke & Los H ..6J 11
Cop La. Pen ............7F 7
Copper Beeches. Pen ....4H 11
Copperwood Way. Chor ...1D 24
Coppice Clo. Chor ......6J 21
Coppice, The. Ing ......7E 2
Coppull Enterprise Cen.
  Cop .................6C 24
Coppull Hall La. Cop ...7E 24
Coppull Rd. Chor .......5D 24
Copse, The. Chor .......4F 25
Copthurst La.
  H'pey & Whit W ......1J 21
Corncroft. Pen .........2G 11
Cornfield. Cot .........5C 2
Cornflower Clo. Chor ...5H 21
Cornthwaite Rd. Ful ....1J 7
Coronation Cres. Pres ..5B 8
Corporation St. Chor ...6H 21
Corporation St. Pres ...4K 7
Cotswold Av. Eux .......6B 20
Cotswold Clo. E'ston ...2F 23
Cotswold Ho. Chor ......2G 25
Cotswold Rd. Chor ......2G 25
Cottage Fields. Chor ...4F 25
Cottage La. Bam B ......3F 13
Cottam Av. Ing .........7D 2
Cottam Grn. Cot ........5C 2
Cottam Hall La. Cot ....6C 2
Cottam La. Ing & Ash R ..1E 6
Cottam La. Longt .......7A 10
Cottam St. Chor ........2G 25
Cottam Way. Cot ........7A 2
Cotton Ct. Pres ........4A 8
Countess Way. Bam B ....4E 12
Countess Way. Eux ......5B 20
Country Clo. Ley .......2J 15
Coupe Grn. Hogh ........1K 13
Court, The. Ful ........4G 3
Court, The. Pen ........1G 11
Coventry St. Chor ......2G 25
Cow La. Ley ............6H 15
Cowley Rd. Rib .........1E 8
Cowling Brow. Chor .....1J 25
Cowling Brow Ind. Est.
  Chor ................2J 25
Cowling Cotts. Char R ..5B 24
Cowling La. Ley ........5F 15
Cowling Rd. Chor .......2K 25
Cowslip Way. Chor ......5H 21
Cow Well La. Whit W ....6F 17
Crabtree Av. Pen .......2E 10
Cragg's Row. Pres ......3K 7
Craigflower Ct. Bam B ..6J 13
Cranbourne St. Pres ....4C 8
Cranbourne Dri. Chor ...1J 25
Cranbourne St. Bam B ...5E 12
Cranbourne St. Chor ....1H 25
Craven Clo. Ful ........4K 3
Crawford Av. Chor ......1F 25

Crawford Av.—Elliott Clo.


Crawford Av. Ley 6J 15
Crawford Av. Pres 3F 9
Crescent St. Pres 3C 8
Crescent, The. Ash R 2E 6
Crescent, The. Bam B 3F 13
Crescent, The. Chor 5G 21
Crescent, The. Lea 3B 6
Crescent, The. Los H 5C 12
Creswell Av. Ing 1D 6
Cricketers Grn. E'ston 1D 22
Croasdale Av. Rib 7E 4
Crocus Fld. Ley 7J 15
Croft Bank. Pen 2G 11
Crofters Grn. Eux 4A 20
Crofters Grn. Pres 2J 7
Crofters Mdw. Far M 3G 15
Crofters Wlk. Pen 3H 11
Croftgate. Ful 6K 3
Croft Mdw. Bam B 7J 13
Croft Pk. Ley 5A 16
Croft Rd. Chor 1J 25
Crofts Dri. Grims 2K 5
Croft St. Pres 4H 7
(in two parts)
Croft, The. E'ston 1E 22
Croft, The. Eux 4K 19
Crombleholme Rd. Pres 3E 8
Cromer Pl. Ing 7E 2
Cromford Wlk. Pres 4C 8
Crompton St. Pres 3C 8
Cromwell Av. Pen 2G 11
Cromwell Rd. Pen 2F 11
Cromwell Rd. Rib 7D 4
Cromwell St. Pres 3A 8
Cromwell Way. Pen 4K 11
Crooked La. Pres 4A 8
Crookings La. Pen 6E 6
Crook St. Chor 3F 25
Crook St. Pres 4B 8
Crosby Pl. Ing 7E 2
Crosier Wlk. Cot 6C 2
Crosse Hall La. Chor 1J 25
Crosse Hall St. Chor 1K 25
Cross Fld. Hut 4A 10
Cross Grn. Rd. Ful 5J 3
Cross Halls. Pen 2F 11
Cross Keys Dri. Whit W 6G 17
Cross St. Chor 6G 21
Cross St. Ley 4K 15
Cross St. Pres 5K 7
Cross Swords Clo. Chor 3F 25
Croston La. Char R 6K 23
Croston Rd.
Far M & Los H 3G 15
Crowell Way. Walt D 2E 12
Crow Hills Rd. Pen 6E 6
Crowle St. Pres 4D 8
Crownlee. Pen 2E 10
Crown St. Chor 7G 21
Crown St. Far 3K 15
Crown St. Pres 4K 7
Crummock Rd. Pres 3G 9
Cub St. Ley 2J 15
(off Country Clo.)
Cuerdale La. Walt D & Sam 7E 8
Cuerden Av. Ley 7F 15
Cuerden Clo. Bam B 2C 16
Cuerden Res. Pk. Ley 3C 16
Cuerden Ri. Los H 6C 12
Cuerden St. Chor 1J 25
Cuerden Valley Pk. 3D 16
Cuerden Way. Bam B 5D 12
Culbeck La. Eux 5H 19
Cumberland Av. Ley 7G 15
Cumberland Ho. Pres 4K 7
(off Warwick St.)
Cunliffe St. Chor 1G 25
Cunliffe St. Pres 4A 8
Cunnery Mdw. Ley 5C 16
Cunningham Av. Chor 2E 24
Curate St. Chor 6J 21
Curlew Clo. Ley 7E 14
Curwen St. Pres 3C 8
(in two parts)
Customs Way. Ash R 4G 7
Cutt Clo. Ley 1B 18
Cuttle St. Pres 4D 8
Cyclamen Clo. Ley 4C 16
Cyon Clo. Pen 7J 7
Cypress Clo. Ley 4C 16
Cypress Clo. Rib 7G 5
Cypress Gro. Los H 5B 12


## D


Dacca St. Chor 6H 21
Dacre Way. Cot 6B 2
Dahlia Clo. Ley 4C 16
Daisy Bank Clo. Ley 5F 15
Daisy Cft. Lea 4B 6
Daisyfields. High B 4D 2
Daisy Fold. Chor 5J 21
Daisy Hill Fold. Eux 6B 20
Daisy La. Pres 1C 8
Daisy Mdw. Bam B 7G 13
Dakin St. Chor 1H 25
Dalby Clo. Pres 1D 8
Dale Av. Eux 6B 20
Dalehead Rd. Ley 7J 15
Dale St. Pres 4B 8
Daleview. Chor 4G 25
Dallas St. Pres 1J 7
Dalmore Rd. Ing 1E 6
Dane Hall La. Eux 5F 19
Danes Dri. Walt D 4D 12
Danesway. Hth C 7K 25
Danesway. Pen 1E 10
Danesway. Walt D 3D 12
(in two parts)
Danewerk St. Pres 4A 8
Darkinson La. Cot 7A 2
Darkinson La. Lea T 1A 6
Dark La. Whit W 2J 21
Darlington St. Cop 7B 24
Dart St. Ash R 4G 7
Darwen St. High W 1H 13
Darwen St. Pres 5C 8
Darwen Vw. Walt D 7E 8
Daub Hall La. Hogh 4K 13
Dawber's La. Eux 5F 19
Dawlish Pl. Ing 1E 6
Dawnay Rd. Rib 1E 8
Dawson La. Ley & Whit W 7B 16
Dawson Pl. Bam B 6G 13
Dawson Wlk. Pres 3K 7
Dean Ct. Bam B 4E 12
Dean St. Bam B 4E 12
Dean Wood Clo. Chor 2E 24
Deborah Av. Ful 4A 4
Deepdale Mill St. Pres 3B 8
Deepdale Retail Pk. Pres 1C 8
Deepdale Rd. Pres & Ful 4B 8
Deepdale St. Pres 4B 8
Deerfold. Chor 5F 21
Deighton Av. Ley 6J 15
Deighton Rd. Chor 2F 25
De Lacy St. Ash R 2H 7
Delamere Pl. Chor 7H 21
Delaware St. Pres 3C 8
Dell, The. Ful 4H 3
Dellway, The. Hut 2B 10
Delph La. Char R 2A 24
(in two parts)
Delph Way. Whit W 7G 17
Demming Clo. Lea 4A 6
Denbigh Clo. Ley 5K 15
Denbigh Way. Pres 5A 8
Denby Clo. Los H 2C 12
Denford Av. Ley 6K 15
Denham La. Brin 5H 17
Denham Wood Clo. Chor 2D 24
Denville Rd. Pres 3C 8
Derby Rd. Ful 7J 3
Derby Sq. Pres 4D 8
Derby St. Ley 4K 15
Derby St. Pres 4A 8
Derek Rd. Whit W 5G 17
Derry Rd. Rib 1E 8
Derwent Hall. Pres 3J 7
(off Ashmoor St.)
Derwent Ho. Pres 4D 8
Derwent Rd. Chor 3F 25
Derwentwater Pl. Pres 2K 7
Dever Av. Ley 5F 15
Devon Clo. Walt D 2D 12
Devon Ct. Pres 3D 8
Devonport Clo. Walt D 2E 12
Devonport Way. Chor 1J 25
Devonport Way Flats. Chor 7J 21
Devonshire Ct. Chor 1G 25
Devonshire Pl. Pres 3E 8
Devonshire Rd. Chor 1G 25
Devonshire Rd. Ful 7A 4
Dewhurst Ind. Est. Pres 3H 7
Dewhurst Row. Bam B 6D 12
Dewhurst St. Pres 3H 7
Dickensons Fld. Pen 3J 11
Dickens Rd. Cop 7C 24
Dickson Av. Pres 2D 8
Dickson Hey. New L 5D 10
Dickson St. Pres 5B 8
Dingle, The. Ful 4H 3
Dingle, The. H'pey 4K 21
Dixons La. Grims 1J 5
Dob Brow. Char R 4C 24
Doctor's La. E'ston 2C 22
Dodd Way. Bam B 7G 13
Dodgson Pl. Pres 3C 8
Dodgson Rd. Pres 3C 8
Dodney Dri. Lea 3A 6
Dog Kennel Wood Nature Reserve.
2C 12
Dole La. Chor 7G 21
Doll La. Ley 5C 14
Dolphin Brow. Whit W 7F 17
Doodstone Av. Los H 4B 12
Doodstone Clo. Los H 4B 12
Doodstone Dri. Los H 4B 12
Doodstone Nook. Los H 4B 12
Dorchester Av. Walt D 3B 12
Doris St. Chor 6H 21
Dorking Rd. Chor 3K 21
Dorman Clo. Ash R 2G 7
Dorman Rd. Rib 1E 8
Dorothy Av. Ley 5J 15
Dorset Av. Walt D 2D 12
Dorset Rd. Pres 3A 8
Douglas Clo. Bam B 5F 13
Douglas Ct. Ful 1H 7
Douglas Ho. Chor 3F 25
Douglas La. Grims 2K 5
Douglas Pl. Chor 3F 25
Douglas Rd. Ful 1H 7
Douglas Rd. N. Ful 1H 7
Douglas St. Ash R 3G 7
Doultons, The. Los H 2C 12
Dove Av. Pen 1J 11
Dovecote. Clay W 3E 16
Dovedale Av. Ing 7E 2
Dovedale Clo. Ing 7E 2
Dovedale Clo. Ley 1J 19
Dovedale Ho. Ful 7E 2
Dove St. Pres 3B 8
Dovetree Clo. Walt D 2A 12
Downham Pl. Ash R 2C 6
Downham Rd. Ley 6E 14
Downing Ct. Brough 1G 3
Downing St. Pres 4E 8
Drakes Cft. Ash R 1G 7
Drakes Hollow. Walt D 1D 12
Draper Av. E'ston 2E 22
Draperfield. Chor 4E 24
Driscoll St. Pres 4B 8
Drive, The. Ful 7A 4
Drive, The. Walt D 7F 9
Drumacre La. E. Longt 7A 10
Drumacre La. W. Longt 7A 10
Drumhead Rd. Chor 4H 21
Duchy Av. Ful 7B 4
Ducie Pl. Pres 3F 9
Duck La. Ful 7H 3
Duddle La. Walt D 4D 12
Dudley Pl. Ash R 2D 6
Dukes Mdw. Ing 6E 2
Duke St. Bam B 6E 12
Duke St. Chor 2G 25
Duke St. Pres 5B 8
Dunbar Dri. Ful 7H 3
Dunbar Rd. Ing 1D 6
Dundonald St. Pres 4D 8
Dunham Dri. Whit W 2G 21
Dunkirk Av. Ful 7G 3
Dunkirk La. Ley 5B 14
Dunmore St. Pres 4B 8
Dunnocks La. Cot 7C 2
Dunoon Clo. Ing 7D 2
Dunrobin Dri. Eux 6B 20
Dunscar Dri. Chor 6J 21
Dunsop Clo. Bam B 5F 13
Dunsop Rd. Rib 7D 4
Durham Clo. Ley 1G 19
Durham Ho. Pres 6A 8
(off Guildford Ho.)
Durton La. Brough 2H 3
(in two parts)
Dutch Barn Clo. Chor 5F 21
Duttonfield Clo. Far M 3G 15
Duxbury Hall Rd. Chor 5J 25
Duxbury Pk. Bus. Cen. Chor 5H 25
Duxbury Pk. Golf Course. 5H 25
Dymock Rd. Pres 3D 8


## E


Eagletown Way. Pen 3A 12
Ealing Gro. Chor 3K 21
Earls Av. Bam B 5E 12
Earl St. Pres 4K 7
Earls Way. Eux 5B 20
Earnshaw Dri. Ley 5F 15
Eastbourne Clo. Ing 6D 2
E. Chorley Bus. Cen. Chor 7H 21
East Cliff. Pres 6K 7
E. Cliff Rd. Pres 6K 7
East Dri. Eux 3B 20
Eastgate. Ful 6J 3
Eastham St. Pres 3J 7
Eastlands. Ley 7E 14
Easton Clo. Ful 5D 4
East Rd. Ful 1A 8
East St. Bam B 6E 12
East St. Far 4K 15
East St. Ley 5K 15
East St. Pres 4A 8
East Vw. Ful 6F 5
East Vw. Los H 6A 12
East Vw. Pres 4A 8
East Vw. Walt D 6C 8
Eastway. Ful 3G 3
Eastway Bus. Village. Ful 3B 4
E. Way La. Chor 7H 21
Eastwood Rd. Ley 5H 15
Eaton Av. Eux 7B 16
Eaves Grn. Rd. Chor 3F 25
Eavesham Clo. Pen 4A 12
Eaves La. Chor 6J 21
Eaves La. Ful 1J 7
Eaveswood Clo. Bam B 4E 12
Eccles St. Pres 3C 8
Ecroyd Rd. Ash R 2G 7
Ecroyd St. Ley 5J 15
Edale Clo. Ley 7J 15
Edale Ct. Pres 3K 7
Eden Hall. Pres 3J 7
(off Ashmoor St.)
Eden St. Ley 6J 15
Edenway. Ful 4H 3
Edgefield. Chor 5F 21
Edgehill Clo. Ful 7J 3
Edgehill Cres. Ley 4G 15
Edgehill Dri. Ful 7H 3
Edinburgh Clo. Ley 5A 16
Edleston Lodge. Rib 7F 5
(off Grange Av.)
Edmund St. Pres 4B 8
Edward VIII Quay. Ash R 4F 7
Edward Sq. Pres 3A 8
Edward St. Bam B 5E 12
Edward St. Chor 1H 25
Edward St. Ley 6J 15
Edward St. Pres 4J 7
Edward St. Walt D 7C 8
Egan St. Pres 4A 8
Egbert St. Pres 3A 8
Egerton Ct. Ash R 3F 7
Egerton Gro. Chor 2F 25
Egerton Rd. Ash R 3E 6
Egerton Rd. Ley 4H 15
Elbow St. Chor 1G 25
Elcho St. Pres 2A 8
Elder Clo. Ful 5D 4
Elder Clo. Whit W 4G 17
Eldon Ho. Chor 1H 25
Eldon St. Ash R & Pres 2G 7
Eldon St. Chor 1H 25
Elgin St. Pres 2A 8
Elijah St. Pres 4D 8
Elizabeth Sq. Pres 3A 8
Elizabeth St. Pres 4K 7
Ellen Ct. Pres 2K 7
Ellen St. Bam B 4E 12
Ellen St. Pres 3H 7
(in three parts)
Ellerbeck Av. Rib 6E 4
Eller Brook Clo. Hth C 7K 25
Ellerslie Rd. Ash R 3F 7
Elliott Clo. Pres 2J 7


30 A-Z Preston

Elliott St. *Pres* . . . . . . . . . . . . .2J **7**
(in two parts)
Elliott Wlk. *Pres* . . . . . . . . . . . .2J **7**
Elm Av. *Ash R* . . . . . . . . . . . . .2D **6**
Elm Dri. *Bam B* . . . . . . . . . . . .4F **13**
Elmfield Dri. *Bam B* . . . . . . . .7J **13**
Elm Gro. *Chor* . . . . . . . . . . . . .5J **21**
Elm Gro. *Ley* . . . . . . . . . . . . . .3B **16**
Elm Gro. *Rib* . . . . . . . . . . . . . . .2E **8**
Elmsett Rd. *Walt D* . . . . . . . . .2F **13**
Elmsley St. *Pres* . . . . . . . . . . .1J **7**
Elms, The. *Clay W* . . . . . . . . .5G **17**
Elmwood. *Chor* . . . . . . . . . . . .6F **21**
Elmwood Av. *Ley* . . . . . . . . . . .5G **15**
Elmwood Dri. *Pen* . . . . . . . . . .1F **11**
Elston Lodge. *Rib* . . . . . . . . . .7F **5**
(off Grange Av.)
Elswick Rd. *Ash R* . . . . . . . . . .3C **6**
Elswick Rd. *Pres* . . . . . . . . . . .6F **15**
Elton St. *Ash R* . . . . . . . . . . . .3G **7**
Emerson Rd. *Pres* . . . . . . . . . .2D **8**
Emily St. *Chor* . . . . . . . . . . . . .3F **25**
Emily St. *Los H* . . . . . . . . . . . .5A **12**
Emmanuel St. *Pres* . . . . . . . . .2J **7**
(in two parts)
Emmett St. *Pres* . . . . . . . . . . . .3K **7**
Emnie La. *Ley* . . . . . . . . . . . . .7E **14**
Empress Av. *Ful* . . . . . . . . . . . .7J **3**
Empress Way. *Eux* . . . . . . . . .5C **20**
Endeavour Clo. *Ash R* . . . . . .5F **7**
Enfield Clo. *E'ston* . . . . . . . . .3E **22**
English Martyrs Pl. *Pres* . . . . .2K **7**
Ennerdale Clo. *Ley* . . . . . . . . .7J **15**
Ennerdale Dri. *Walt D* . . . . . . .7E **8**
Ennerdale Rd. *Chor* . . . . . . . .2E **24**
Enterprise Dri. *Ley* . . . . . . . . .1H **15**
Ephraim St. *Pres* . . . . . . . . . . .5C **8**
Epping Pl. *Chor* . . . . . . . . . . . .7H **21**
Epsom Clo. *Chor* . . . . . . . . . . .3K **21**
Erskine Rd. *Chor* . . . . . . . . . . .6J **21**
Esher Pond. *Ful* . . . . . . . . . . . .5G **3**
Eskdale Clo. *Chor* . . . . . . . . . .3K **3**
Eskdale Rd. *Ley* . . . . . . . . . . .7A **16**
Esplanade. *Pres* . . . . . . . . . . .7B **8**
Essex St. *Pres* . . . . . . . . . . . . .3A **8**
Eton Pk. *Ful* . . . . . . . . . . . . . . .6C **4**
Europa Dri. *Ley* . . . . . . . . . . . .1J **15**
Euston St. *Pres* . . . . . . . . . . . .5J **7**
Euxton Hall Ct. *Eux* . . . . . . . . .5A **20**
Euxton Hall Gdns. *Eux* . . . . . .5A **20**
Euxton Hall M. *Eux* . . . . . . . . .5A **20**
Euxton La. *Chor & Eux* . . . . . .3B **20**
Euxton Pk. Golf Cen. . . . . . . . .3E **20**
Evans St. *Ash R* . . . . . . . . . . . .3H **7**
Evergreen Av. *Ley* . . . . . . . . . .7J **15**
Evergreen Clo. *Chor* . . . . . . . .3F **25**
Evergreens, The. *Cot* . . . . . . . .7C **2**
Eversleigh St. *Pres* . . . . . . . . .3J **7**
Evesham Av. *Pen* . . . . . . . . . . .3J **11**
Evesham Clo. *Hut* . . . . . . . . . .4A **10**
Ewell Clo. *Chor* . . . . . . . . . . . .3K **21**
Exe St. *Pres* . . . . . . . . . . . . . . .2B **8**
Exeter Pl. *Ash R* . . . . . . . . . . .2C **6**

**F**

Factory La. *Pen* . . . . . . . . . . . .2J **11**
Factory La. *Whit W* . . . . . . . . .6F **17**
Fairfax Pl. *Walt D* . . . . . . . . . .3D **12**
Fairfax Rd. *Rib* . . . . . . . . . . . . .7E **4**
Fairfield Dri. *Ash R* . . . . . . . . .2F **7**
Fairfield Rd. *Ful* . . . . . . . . . . . .7A **4**
Fairfield Rd. *Ley* . . . . . . . . . . .6H **15**
Fairfield St. *Los H* . . . . . . . . . .6B **12**
Fairham Av. *Pen* . . . . . . . . . . .3H **11**
Fairhaven Rd. *Ley* . . . . . . . . . .5F **15**
Fairhaven Rd. *Pen* . . . . . . . . . .7J **7**
Fair Oak Clo. *Rib* . . . . . . . . . . .1F **9**
Fairview Dri. *Hth C* . . . . . . . . .7K **25**
Fairway. *Chor* . . . . . . . . . . . . . .5G **21**
Fairway. *Pen* . . . . . . . . . . . . . . .6F **7**
Fairways. *Ful* . . . . . . . . . . . . . . .5A **4**
Fairways Av. *Brough* . . . . . . . .1G **3**
Falcon St. *Pres* . . . . . . . . . . . . .2B **8**
Falkland St. *Pres* . . . . . . . . . . .5J **7**
Faraday Dri. *Ful* . . . . . . . . . . . .4C **4**
Far Cft. *Los H* . . . . . . . . . . . . .4A **12**
Fareham Clo. *Ful* . . . . . . . . . . .7A **4**
Fareham Clo. *Walt D* . . . . . . . .2F **13**
Far Fld. *Pen* . . . . . . . . . . . . . . .1H **11**
Farington Av. *Ley* . . . . . . . . . . .7F **15**

Farington Bus. Pk. *Ley* . . . . . .2J **15**
Farington Ga. *Ley* . . . . . . . . . .4K **15**
**Farington Lodges Nature Reserve.**
. . . . . . . . . . . . . . . . . . . . . . . . . .6J **11**
Farington Rd.
*Far M & Los H* . . . . . . .7K **11**
Far La. *Pen* . . . . . . . . . . . . . . .3G **11**
Farm Av. *Adl* . . . . . . . . . . . . . .7K **25**
Farmend Clo. *Longt* . . . . . . . . .5A **10**
Farmhouse Clo. *Whit W* . . . . .1G **21**
Far Nook. *Whit W* . . . . . . . . . .7F **17**
Farringdon Clo. *Pres* . . . . . . . .3F **9**
Farringdon Cres. *Pres* . . . . . .3F **9**
Farringdon La. *Rib* . . . . . . . . . .1F **9**
Farringdon Pl. *Pres* . . . . . . . . .3F **9**
Farrington St. *Chor* . . . . . . . . .7G **21**
Farthings, The. *Chor* . . . . . . . .6D **20**
Fazackerley St. *Ash R* . . . . . .3G **7**
Fazakerley St. *Chor* . . . . . . . . .7G **21**
Fell Clo. *Bam B* . . . . . . . . . . . .5F **13**
Fellery St. *Chor* . . . . . . . . . . . .7G **21**
Fell Vw. *Chor* . . . . . . . . . . . . . .2J **25**
Fell Vw. *Grims* . . . . . . . . . . . . .1J **5**
Fellway Clo. *Los H* . . . . . . . . . .5C **12**
Felstead St. *Pres* . . . . . . . . . . .4D **8**
Fensway. *Hut* . . . . . . . . . . . . . .3B **10**
Fenton Rd. *Ful* . . . . . . . . . . . . .7C **4**
Fermor Rd. *Pres* . . . . . . . . . . .3E **8**
Fernbank. *Chor* . . . . . . . . . . . . .4H **21**
Fern Clo. *Los H* . . . . . . . . . . . .5B **12**
Ferndale Clo. *Ley* . . . . . . . . . .7K **15**
Fernleigh. *Ley* . . . . . . . . . . . . .6C **14**
Fern Mdw. *Whit W* . . . . . . . . . .3G **17**
Ferns, The. *Ash R* . . . . . . . . . .2G **7**
Ferns, The. *Walt D* . . . . . . . . . .2B **12**
Fernyhalgh Ct. *Ful* . . . . . . . . . .5D **4**
Fernyhalgh Gdns. *Ful* . . . . . . .5D **4**
Fernyhalgh Gro. *Ful* . . . . . . . . .5D **4**
Fernyhalgh La. *Ful* . . . . . . . . . .2C **4**
(in two parts)
Fernyhalgh Pl. *Ful* . . . . . . . . . .5D **4**
Ferry Rd. *Ash R* . . . . . . . . . . . .4D **6**
Fiddlers La. *Clay W* . . . . . . . . .4F **17**
Fidler La. *Far M* . . . . . . . . . . . .1H **15**
Fielden St. *Chor* . . . . . . . . . . . .7J **21**
Fielden St. *Ley* . . . . . . . . . . . . .5F **15**
Fieldfare Ct. *Chor* . . . . . . . . . .3D **24**
Fieldings, The. *Ful* . . . . . . . . . .1H **7**
Fld. Maple Dri. *Rib* . . . . . . . . . .1F **9**
Fld. Rose Ct. *Hth C* . . . . . . . . .7K **25**
Fieldside Av. *Eux* . . . . . . . . . . .6A **20**
Fieldside Clo. *Los H* . . . . . . . .2C **12**
Fields, The. *E'ston* . . . . . . . . . .1D **22**
Fife Clo. *Chor* . . . . . . . . . . . . . .2J **25**
Filberts Clo. *Ful* . . . . . . . . . . . .1G **7**
Filberts, The. *Ful* . . . . . . . . . . .1G **7**
File St. *Chor* . . . . . . . . . . . . . . .1G **25**
Filey Pl. *Ing* . . . . . . . . . . . . . . . .7E **2**
Finch La. *Cot* . . . . . . . . . . . . . . .7C **2**
Finch's Cotts. *Pen* . . . . . . . . . .1J **11**
Firbank. *Bam B* . . . . . . . . . . . .4D **12**
Firbank. *Eux* . . . . . . . . . . . . . . .5A **20**
First Av. *Ash R* . . . . . . . . . . . . .2E **6**
Fir Tree Av. *Ful* . . . . . . . . . . . . .7F **3**
Fir Tree Clo. *Chor* . . . . . . . . . .5G **25**
Fir Trees Av. *Los H* . . . . . . . . .4A **12**
Fir Trees Av. *Rib* . . . . . . . . . . . .7F **5**
Fir Trees Cres. *Los H* . . . . . . .5A **12**
Fir Trees Pl. *Rib* . . . . . . . . . . . .7F **5**
Fir Trees Rd. *Los H* . . . . . . . . .4A **12**
Fishergate. *Pres* . . . . . . . . . . . .5J **7**
Fishergate Cen. *Pres* . . . . . . .5K **7**
Fishergate Ct. *Pres* . . . . . . . . .5J **7**
Fishergate Hill. *Pres* . . . . . . . . .6H **7**
Fishergate Wlk. *Pres* . . . . . . . .5K **7**
Fish St. *Pres* . . . . . . . . . . . . . . .3K **7**
Fishwick Bottoms. *Pres* . . . . . .6C **8**
**Fishwick Hall Golf Course.** . .4F **9**
Fishwick Pde. *Pres* . . . . . . . . .4C **8**
Fishwick Rd. *Pres* . . . . . . . . . .4C **8**
Fishwick Vw. *Pres* . . . . . . . . . .4C **8**
Fitchfield. *Pen* . . . . . . . . . . . . . .3K **11**
Fitzgerald St. *Pres* . . . . . . . . . .3C **8**
Fitzroy St. *Pres* . . . . . . . . . . . . .5H **7**
Five Acres. *Far M* . . . . . . . . . .2G **15**
Flag La. *Hth C* . . . . . . . . . . . . .3K **25**
Flag La. *Ley & Eux* . . . . . . . . .3F **19**
Flag La. *Pen* . . . . . . . . . . . . . . .4K **11**
Flats Retail Pk., The. *Walt D* . .7C **8**
Flats, The. *Chor* . . . . . . . . . . . .2F **25**
Fleet St. *Chor* . . . . . . . . . . . . . .1G **25**
Fleet St. *Pres* . . . . . . . . . . . . . .5K **7**

Fleetwood St. *Ash R* . . . . . . . .3H **7**
Fleetwood St. *Ley* . . . . . . . . . .4K **15**
Flensburg Way. *Ley* . . . . . . . . .3F **15**
Fletcher Rd. *Pres* . . . . . . . . . . .4B **8**
Flett St. *Ash R* . . . . . . . . . . . . .3G **7**
Flintoff Way. *Pres* . . . . . . . . . . .1B **8**
Flowerfield. *Cot* . . . . . . . . . . . .5C **2**
Floyd Rd. *Rib* . . . . . . . . . . . . . .1E **8**
Floyer St. *Pres* . . . . . . . . . . . . .5B **8**
Folly Wood Dri. *Chor* . . . . . . . .2E **24**
Foregate. *Ful* . . . . . . . . . . . . . . .7J **3**
Forest Brook Ho. *Ful* . . . . . . . .1K **7**
Forest Clo. *Los H* . . . . . . . . . .2C **12**
Forest Way. *Ful* . . . . . . . . . . . . .6K **3**
Forest Way. *Ley* . . . . . . . . . . . .6H **15**
Forge St. *Ley* . . . . . . . . . . . . . .5J **15**
Formby Pl. *Ash R* . . . . . . . . . . .2C **6**
(in two parts)
Forrester Clo. *Ley* . . . . . . . . . .5G **15**
Forshaw Rd. *Pen* . . . . . . . . . . .3H **11**
Forsythia Dri. *Clay W* . . . . . . .2F **17**
Forton Rd. *Ash R* . . . . . . . . . . .4C **6**
Forward Ind. Est. *Ley* . . . . . . .4G **15**
(off Talbot Rd.)
Fossdale Moss. *Ley* . . . . . . . . .5E **14**
Foster Cft. *Pen* . . . . . . . . . . . . .6G **7**
Fosterfield Pl. *Chor* . . . . . . . . .6J **21**
Foster St. *Chor* . . . . . . . . . . . . .6J **21**
Foundary St. *Chor* . . . . . . . . . .7G **21**
Fountains Clo. *Chor* . . . . . . . . .3H **25**
Fountains Reach. *Walt D* . . . . .4D **12**
Fourfields. *Bam B* . . . . . . . . . . .3E **12**
Four Oaks Rd. *Bam B* . . . . . . .7G **13**
Fowler Av. *Far M* . . . . . . . . . . .7B **12**
Fowler La. *Far & Far M* . . . . . .7K **11**
Fowler St. *Ful* . . . . . . . . . . . . . .1H **7**
Foxcote. *Chor* . . . . . . . . . . . . . .5F **21**
Foxdale Gro. *Pres* . . . . . . . . . .1D **8**
Foxglove Dri. *Whit W* . . . . . . . .2F **21**
Foxhole Rd. *Chor* . . . . . . . . . . .6D **20**
Fox La. *Ley* . . . . . . . . . . . . . . . .6F **15**
Fox St. *Pres* . . . . . . . . . . . . . . .5K **7**
Foxwood, The. *Char R* . . . . . . .7A **24**
Francis St. *Ash R* . . . . . . . . . . .3G **7**
Frankel Clo. *New L* . . . . . . . . . .5D **10**
Franklands Dri. *Rib* . . . . . . . . . .6F **5**
Frank St. *Pres* . . . . . . . . . . . . . .3K **7**
Fraser Av. *Pen* . . . . . . . . . . . . .7J **7**
Frederick St. *Chor* . . . . . . . . . .1J **25**
Freeman's La. *Char R* . . . . . . .5C **24**
Frenchwood Av. *Pres* . . . . . . . .6B **8**
Frenchwood Knoll. *Pres* . . . . . .6B **8**
Frenchwood St. *Pres* . . . . . . . .6A **8**
Freshfields. *Lea* . . . . . . . . . . . .1B **6**
Friargate. *Pres* . . . . . . . . . . . . .4K **7**
Friargate Wlk. *Pres* . . . . . . . . .5K **7**
Friars, The. *Ful* . . . . . . . . . . . . .7J **3**
Friday St. *Chor* . . . . . . . . . . . . .7H **21**
Frome St. *Pres* . . . . . . . . . . . . .3D **8**
Froom St. *Chor* . . . . . . . . . . . . .1H **25**
(in two parts)
Fryer Clo. *Pen* . . . . . . . . . . . . . .4G **11**
Fulford Av. *Lea* . . . . . . . . . . . . .3A **6**
Fulshaw Rd. *Ash R* . . . . . . . . .2F **7**
Fulwood Hall La. *Ful* . . . . . . . . .7B **4**
Fulwood Heights. *Ful* . . . . . . . .6C **4**
Fulwood Pk. *Ful* . . . . . . . . . . . .4B **4**
Fulwood Row. *Ful & Rib* . . . . . .4E **4**
(in two parts)
Furness Clo. *Chor* . . . . . . . . . .3H **25**
Fylde Av. *Far M* . . . . . . . . . . . .2G **15**
Fylde Av. *Ash R & Pres* . . . . . .3H **7**
Fylde Rd. Ind. Est. *Pres* . . . . .3H **7**
Fylde St. *Pres* . . . . . . . . . . . . . .4J **7**

**G**

Gables, The. *Cot* . . . . . . . . . . . .7C **2**
Gainsborough Av. *Los H* . . . . .6A **12**
Gamull La. *Rib* . . . . . . . . . . . . .6F **5**
Ganton Ct. *Pen* . . . . . . . . . . . . .6E **6**
Garden Ct. *Ash R* . . . . . . . . . . .3G **7**
(off Tulketh Av.)
Gardenia Clo. *Clay W* . . . . . . .2F **17**
Garden St. *Los H* . . . . . . . . . . .6B **12**
Garden St. *Pres* . . . . . . . . . . . .5K **7**
Garden Ter. *Chor* . . . . . . . . . . .6G **21**
Garden Wlk. *Ash R* . . . . . . . . . .3F **7**
Gardner St. *Pres* . . . . . . . . . . . .4K **7**
Garfield Ter. *Chor* . . . . . . . . . . .5H **21**
Garforth Cres. *Bam B* . . . . . . .4E **12**

Garrison Rd. *Ful* . . . . . . . . . . . .1B **8**
Garsdale Clo. *Walt D* . . . . . . . .7E **8**
Garsdale Rd. *Rib* . . . . . . . . . . .7E **4**
Garstang Rd. *Brough & Ful* . . .1G **3**
(in two parts)
Garstang Rd. *Ful & Pres* . . . . .1J **7**
Garstone Cft. *Ful* . . . . . . . . . . . .5G **3**
Gaskell Rd. *Pen* . . . . . . . . . . . .7J **7**
Gaskell St. *Chor* . . . . . . . . . . . .7J **21**
Gas Ter. *Ley* . . . . . . . . . . . . . . .4J **15**
Gatesgarth Av. *Ful* . . . . . . . . . .4K **3**
Gathurst Rd. *Ash R* . . . . . . . . .2G **7**
Gaythorne Av. *Pres* . . . . . . . . .3F **9**
Geneva Rd. *Ful* . . . . . . . . . . . . .7C **4**
Geoffrey St. *Chor* . . . . . . . . . . .6H **21**
Geoffrey St. *Pres* . . . . . . . . . . .3C **8**
Georges Rd. *Pres* . . . . . . . . . .5K **7**
George St. *Chor* . . . . . . . . . . . .1G **25**
George St. *Ley* . . . . . . . . . . . . .4K **15**
George St. *Pres* . . . . . . . . . . . .5B **8**
German La. *Char R* . . . . . . . . .7B **20**
German La. *Cop* . . . . . . . . . . . .7C **24**
Gerrard St. *Pres* . . . . . . . . . . . .5H **7**
Gilbertson Rd. *Hth C* . . . . . . . .6J **25**
Gilbert St. *Chor* . . . . . . . . . . . .2G **25**
Gildow St. *Pres* . . . . . . . . . . . . .4J **7**
Gilhouse Av. *Lea* . . . . . . . . . . .3A **6**
Gillcroft. *E'ston* . . . . . . . . . . . . .1D **22**
Giller Clo. *Pen* . . . . . . . . . . . . .3J **11**
Giller Dri. *Pen* . . . . . . . . . . . . . .3J **11**
Giller Fold. *Pen* . . . . . . . . . . . . .3K **11**
Gillett St. *Pres* . . . . . . . . . . . . . .3C **8**
(in two parts)
Gillibrand Clo. *Pen* . . . . . . . . . .4G **11**
Gillibrand Ho. *Chor* . . . . . . . . . .5G **21**
(off Lancaster Ct.)
Gillibrand St. *Chor* . . . . . . . . . .1G **25**
Gillibrand St. *Walt D* . . . . . . . . .7D **8**
Gillibrand Walks. *Chor* . . . . . . .2F **25**
Gill La. *Longt* . . . . . . . . . . . . . . .1A **14**
Gin Bow. *Chor* . . . . . . . . . . . . .2H **25**
Ginnel, The. *Ley* . . . . . . . . . . . .6J **15**
Gisburn Rd. *Rib* . . . . . . . . . . . .7E **4**
Glamis Dri. *Chor* . . . . . . . . . . . .7E **20**
Glamis Rd. *Ley* . . . . . . . . . . . . .6A **16**
Glebe Clo. *Ful* . . . . . . . . . . . . . .7K **3**
Glebe, The. *Ley* . . . . . . . . . . . .6F **15**
Glencourse Dri. *Ful* . . . . . . . . . .6C **4**
Glencroft. *Eux* . . . . . . . . . . . . . .4K **19**
Glendale Av. *Los H* . . . . . . . . .4C **12**
Glendale Clo. *Ley* . . . . . . . . . . .7K **15**
Glendale Cres. *Los H* . . . . . . .4C **12**
Glendale Gro. *Rib* . . . . . . . . . . .2D **8**
Gleneagles Dri. *Eux* . . . . . . . . .3B **20**
Gleneagles Dri. *Ful* . . . . . . . . . .4F **3**
Gleneagles Dri. *Pen* . . . . . . . . .6E **6**
Glen Gro. *Rib* . . . . . . . . . . . . . .6F **5**
Glenluce Dri. *Pres* . . . . . . . . . . .4F **9**
Glenmore. *Clay W* . . . . . . . . . .3E **16**
Glen, The. *Rib* . . . . . . . . . . . . . .2F **9**
Glenview Clo. *Rib* . . . . . . . . . . .1G **9**
Glenview Ct. *Rib* . . . . . . . . . . . .1G **9**
(in two parts)
Glenway. *Pen* . . . . . . . . . . . . . .1G **11**
Gloucester Av. *Far* . . . . . . . . . .3A **16**
Gloucester Rd. *Chor* . . . . . . . .3G **25**
Glover Clo. *Ley* . . . . . . . . . . . . .1B **18**
Glovers Ct. *Pres* . . . . . . . . . . . .5K **7**
Glover St. *Pres* . . . . . . . . . . . . .5A **8**
Golbourne St. *Pres* . . . . . . . . . .3B **8**
Goldburn Clo. *Ing* . . . . . . . . . . .5D **2**
Goldcrest Dri. *Bam B* . . . . . . . .3G **13**
Golden Hill. *Pen* . . . . . . . . . . . .4K **15**
Golden Hill La. *Ley* . . . . . . . . . .4G **15**
Golden Way. *Pen* . . . . . . . . . . .3F **11**
Goldfinch Ct. *Chor* . . . . . . . . . .3D **24**
Goldfinch St. *Pres* . . . . . . . . . . .2B **8**
Golf Vw. *Ing* . . . . . . . . . . . . . . . .5E **2**
Goodier St. *Pres* . . . . . . . . . . . .4C **8**
Good St. *Pres* . . . . . . . . . . . . . .5J **7**
Goodwood Av. *Ful* . . . . . . . . . .4K **3**
Goose Grn. Av. *Cop* . . . . . . . . .7D **24**
Gordon St. *Chor* . . . . . . . . . . . .1H **25**
Gordon St. *Pres* . . . . . . . . . . . .3J **7**
(in two parts)
Goring St. *Chor* . . . . . . . . . . . . .1H **25**
Gorse Clo. *Whit W* . . . . . . . . . .2J **21**
Gorse Gro. *Rib* . . . . . . . . . . . . .1E **8**
Gorsewood Rd. *Ley* . . . . . . . . .5G **15**
Gosforth Clo. *Walt D* . . . . . . . .2E **12**
Gough La. *Bam B* . . . . . . . . . . .7H **13**
(in two parts)

Goulding Av. Ley . . . . . . . . .5K 15
Goulding St. Chor . . . . . . . . .2H 25
Gower Ct. Ley . . . . . . . . . . .3F 15
Gradwell St. Pres . . . . . . . . . .4J 7
Grafton Rd. Rib . . . . . . . . . . .7F 5
Grafton St. Chor . . . . . . . . . .3F 25
Grafton St. Pres . . . . . . . . . . .6J 7
Graham Av. Los H . . . . . . . .5C 12
Graham St. Pres . . . . . . . . . .3B 8
Grange Av. Rib . . . . . . . . . . .7F 5
            (in two parts)
Grange Dri. Cop . . . . . . . . . .7B 24
Grange Dri. Eux . . . . . . . . . .3A 20
Grange Dri. Hogh . . . . . . . . .1K 13
Grange Pk. Clo. Pen . . . . . . . .6E 6
Grange Pl. Rib . . . . . . . . . . .7F 5
Grange Rd. Ash R . . . . . . . . .1G 7
Grange Rd. Ley . . . . . . . . . .5F 15
Grange, The. Cot . . . . . . . . . .6B 2
Granings, The. Cot . . . . . . . . .5B 2
Granton Wlk. Ing . . . . . . . . . .7E 2
Granville Ct. Chor . . . . . . . . .6J 21
Granville Rd. Chor . . . . . . . . .6J 21
Grasmere Av. Far . . . . . . . . .3J 15
Grasmere Clo. Eux . . . . . . . .6C 20
Grasmere Clo. Ful . . . . . . . . .7C 4
Grasmere Clo. Walt D . . . . . . .3E 12
Grasmere Gro. Whit W . . . . . .7F 17
Grasmere Ter. Chor . . . . . . . .3F 25
Gt. Avenham St. Pres . . . . . . .6A 8
Gt. George St. Pres . . . . . . . .3A 8
Gt. Greens La. Bam B . . . . . .1F 17
Gt. Hanover St. Pres . . . . . . . .3A 8
Gt. Meadow. Chor . . . . . . . . .5E 20
Gt. Meadow. Los H . . . . . . . .5A 12
Gt. Park Dri. Ley . . . . . . . . . .4J 15
Gt. Shaw St. Pres . . . . . . . . . .4K 7
Gt. Townley St. Pres . . . . . . . .4D 8
Gt. Wood Clo. Chor . . . . . . . .2D 24
Greaves Mdw. Pen . . . . . . . .3K 11
Greaves St. Pres . . . . . . . . . .5A 8
Greaves Town La. Lea . . . . . . .3C 6
Greenacres. Clay W . . . . . . . .3G 17
Greenacres. Chor . . . . . . . . .3G 25
Greenacres. Ful . . . . . . . . . . .4F 3
Greenacres, The. Hut . . . . . . .3B 10
Greenbank Av. Pres . . . . . . . .2H 7
Greenbank Pl. Pres . . . . . . . .3J 7
Greenbank Rd. Pen . . . . . . . .1J 11
Greenbank St. Pres . . . . . . . .2H 7
            (in three parts)
Greencroft. Pen . . . . . . . . . .2H 11
Greendale M. Ash R . . . . . . . .2C 6
Green Dri. Ful . . . . . . . . . . . .4J 3
Green Dri. Los H . . . . . . . . . .4C 12
Green Dri. Pen . . . . . . . . . . . .7F 7
Greenfield Dri. Los H . . . . . . .5A 12
Greenfield Rd. Chor . . . . . . . .7J 21
Greenfield Way. Ing . . . . . . . . .6F 3
Green Ga. Ful . . . . . . . . . . . .1G 7
Green Ga. Hut . . . . . . . . . . .4A 10
Greenlands Cres. Rib . . . . . . .1E 8
Greenlands Gro. Rib . . . . . . . .1E 8
Green La. Far M . . . . . . . . . .6J 11
Green La. Wstke . . . . . . . . . .4G 11
Greenmead Clo. Cot . . . . . . . .6C 2
Green Pl. Bam B . . . . . . . . . .7G 13
Greenside. Cot . . . . . . . . . . . .7B 2
Greenside. Eux . . . . . . . . . .4A 20
Greenside Av. Lea . . . . . . . . .3A 6
Greenside Gdns. Ley . . . . . . .7D 14
Green St. Chor . . . . . . . . . . .3E 24
Greensway. Brough . . . . . . . . .1G 3
Green, The. E'ston . . . . . . . .1D 22
Green, The. Hth C . . . . . . . . .6K 25
Green, The. Rib . . . . . . . . . . .2F 9
Greenthorn Cres. Rib . . . . . . .2G 9
Greenway. E'ston . . . . . . . . .1D 22
Greenway. Ful . . . . . . . . . . . .4H 3
Greenway. Pen . . . . . . . . . . .1F 11
Greenwood. Bam B . . . . . . . .1F 17
Greenwood Ct. Ley . . . . . . . .4J 15
Greenwood St. Bam B . . . . . .4E 12
Greenwood St. Pres . . . . . . . .5B 8
Gregson La. Hogh . . . . . . . . .2H 13
Gregson Way. Ful . . . . . . . . . .6B 4
Grenville Av. Walt D . . . . . . . .3D 12
Greyfriars Av. Ful . . . . . . . . . .6H 3
Greyfriars Cres. Ful . . . . . . . .6H 3
Greyfriars Dri. Pen . . . . . . . . .7G 7
Grey Heights Vw. Chor . . . . . .7J 21
            (in three parts)

Greystock Av. Ful . . . . . . . . . .5J 3
Greystock Clo. Bam B . . . . . .5H 13
Greystock Pl. Ful . . . . . . . . . .5J 3
Greystones. Ley . . . . . . . . . .5D 14
Grimsargh St. Pres . . . . . . . . .3D 8
Grimshaw St. Pres . . . . . . . . .5A 8
Grisedale Pl. Chor . . . . . . . . .3F 25
Grizedale Clo. Rib . . . . . . . . . .2F 9
Grizedale Cres. Rib . . . . . . . . .2F 9
Grizedale Pl. Rib . . . . . . . . . .2F 9
Grosvenor Pl. Ash R . . . . . . . .2F 7
Grosvenor Rd. Chor . . . . . . . .2F 25
Grosvenor St. Pres . . . . . . . . .5B 8
Grove Mill Development Cen.
                . . . . . . . .3E 22
Grove Rd. Walt D . . . . . . . . . .6C 8
Grove St. Bam B . . . . . . . . . .5F 13
Grove St. Ley . . . . . . . . . . . .6F 15
Grove, The. Ash R . . . . . . . . .3F 7
Grove, The. Chor . . . . . . . . . .5G 21
Grove, The. Pen . . . . . . . . . .1F 11
Grundy's La. Chor . . . . . . . . .7G 25
Grundy St. Ley . . . . . . . . . . .4J 15
Guardian Clo. Ful . . . . . . . . . .7A 4
Guernsey Av. Eux . . . . . . . . .1D 20
Guildford Av. Chor . . . . . . . . .3J 21
Guildford Rd. Pres . . . . . . . . .5A 8
Guild Hall . . . . . . . . . . . . . .5A 8
Guild Hall Arc. Pres . . . . . . . .5A 8
            (off Lancaster Rd.)
Guildhall St. Pres . . . . . . . . . .5K 7
Guild Row. Pres . . . . . . . . . .5A 8
Guild Trad. Est. Pres . . . . . . . .3B 8
Guild Way. Pres . . . . . . . . . . .5H 7

# H

Hacklands Av. Lea . . . . . . . . . .3A 6
Haddon Pl. Ful . . . . . . . . . . . .1H 7
Haig Av. Ash R . . . . . . . . . . .2H 7
Haig Av. Ley . . . . . . . . . . . .5H 15
Haigh Clo. Chor . . . . . . . . . .1E 24
Haigh Cres. Chor . . . . . . . . .1E 24
Haighton Ct. Ful . . . . . . . . . .4A 4
Haighton Dri. Ful . . . . . . . . . .6E 4
Haighton Grn. La. Haig . . . . . .2C 4
Half Acre. Los H . . . . . . . . . .5A 12
Halfpenny La. Hesk . . . . . . . .5C 22
Hall Cft. Hut . . . . . . . . . . . .3B 10
Hall Cft. Head. Hut . . . . . . . .3B 10
Hall Ga. Chor . . . . . . . . . . . .6E 20
Hall Grn. La. Hesk . . . . . . . . .5B 22
Halliwell Ct. Chor . . . . . . . . . .1G 25
            (off Halliwell St.)
Halliwell Cres. Hut . . . . . . . . .3C 10
Halliwell Ho. Walt D . . . . . . . .2F 13
Halliwell La. Chor . . . . . . . . .3G 21
Halliwell Pl. Chor . . . . . . . . . .1G 25
Halliwell St. Chor . . . . . . . . . .1G 25
Hall La. Ley . . . . . . . . . . . . .3H 15
Hall La. Maw . . . . . . . . . . . .5A 22
Hall Rd. Ful . . . . . . . . . . . . . .6J 3
Hall Rd. Pen . . . . . . . . . . . .2J 11
Hall St. Ash R . . . . . . . . . . . .3G 7
Hallwood Rd. Chor . . . . . . . . .3E 24
Halsbury St. Pres . . . . . . . . . .6A 8
Halstead Rd. Rib . . . . . . . . . . .6D 4
Halton Av. Ley . . . . . . . . . . .4B 16
Halton Pl. Rib . . . . . . . . . . . .7F 5
Hambleton Dri. Pen . . . . . . . .3J 11
Hamer Rd. Ash R . . . . . . . . . .1H 7
Hamilton Gro. Rib . . . . . . . . . .1E 8
Hamilton Rd. Chor . . . . . . . . .1F 25
Hamilton Rd. Rib . . . . . . . . . .7D 4
Hamlet, The. Hth C . . . . . . . .7K 25
Hammond Ct. Pres . . . . . . . . .3J 7
Hammond's Row. Pres . . . . . . .5A 8
Hammond St. Pres . . . . . . . . .3H 7
            (Bold St., in three parts)
Hammond St. Pres . . . . . . . . .2K 7
            (Garstang Rd.)
Hampden Rd. Ley . . . . . . . . .4J 15
Hampshire Rd. Walt D . . . . . . .2D 12
Hampson Av. Ley . . . . . . . . .5B 16
Hampstead Rd. Rib . . . . . . . . .2D 8
Hampton Clo. Chor . . . . . . . . .7F 21
Hampton St. Ash R . . . . . . . . .2G 7
Hampton St. Ash R . . . . . . . . .3G 7
Handbridge, The. Ful . . . . . . . .6J 3
Hand La. Maw . . . . . . . . . . .3B 22

Handshaw Dri. Pen . . . . . . . .3A 12
Hanover Ct. Ing . . . . . . . . . . .5D 2
Hanover St. Pres . . . . . . . . . .3K 7
Harcourt St. Pres . . . . . . . . . .3J 7
Hardaker St. Whit W . . . . . . . .2F 21
Hardcastle Rd. Ful . . . . . . . . . .1J 7
Hardman's Yd. Pres . . . . . . . .5K 7
Hardwen Av. Lea . . . . . . . . . .3A 6
            (off Dodney Dr.)
Hardwick St. Pres . . . . . . . . . .4A 8
Hardy Clo. Ash R . . . . . . . . . .4D 6
Hardy Dri. Chor . . . . . . . . . .1E 24
Hareden Rd. Rib . . . . . . . . . . .2F 9
Haredon Clo. Bam B . . . . . . . .5F 13
Harestone Av. Chor . . . . . . . .3E 24
Hargreaves Av. Ley . . . . . . . .6K 15
Hargreaves Ct. Ing . . . . . . . . .7D 2
Harland St. Ful . . . . . . . . . . .1H 7
Harlech Dri. Ley . . . . . . . . . .5A 16
Harling Rd. Pres . . . . . . . . . . .3D 8
Harold Ter. Los H . . . . . . . . .5A 12
Harperley. Chor . . . . . . . . . . .5F 21
Harpers La. Chor . . . . . . . . . .6H 21
Harpers St. Chor . . . . . . . . . .5H 21
Harrington Rd. Chor . . . . . . . .7F 21
Harrington St. Pres . . . . . . . . .4K 7
Harris Mus. & Art Gallery. . .5A 8
Harrison La. Hut . . . . . . . . . .3F 11
Harrison Rd. Chor . . . . . . . . .2G 25
Harrison Rd. Ful . . . . . . . . . . .6J 3
Harrison Trad. Est. Pres . . . . . .3C 8
Harris St. Pres . . . . . . . . . . . .5A 8
Harrock Rd. Ley . . . . . . . . . .5B 16
Harrop Pl. Rib . . . . . . . . . . . .7E 4
Hartington Rd. Pres . . . . . . . . .5H 7
Hartwood Grn. Chor . . . . . . . .4H 21
Harvest Dri. Whit W . . . . . . . .1G 21
Haslemere Ind. Est. Ley . . . . .3H 15
Hassett Clo. Pres . . . . . . . . . .6J 7
Hastings Rd. Ash R . . . . . . . . .3F 7
Hastings Rd. Ley . . . . . . . . . .4K 15
Hatfield Rd. Rib . . . . . . . . . . .1E 8
Havelock Rd. Bam B . . . . . . .6E 12
Havelock Rd. Pen . . . . . . . . . .7J 7
Havelock St. Pres . . . . . . . . . .2H 7
            (in four parts)
Hawarden Rd. Pres . . . . . . . . .3E 8
Haweswater Av. Chor . . . . . . .2F 25
Hawkhurst Av. Ful . . . . . . . . . .5H 3
Hawkhurst Cres. Ful . . . . . . . .5H 3
Hawkhurst Rd. Pen . . . . . . . .1J 11
Hawkhurst Rd. Pres . . . . . . . . .2B 8
Hawkins Clo. Pres . . . . . . . . . .3J 7
Hawkins St. Pres . . . . . . . . . .3J 7
            (in two parts)
Hawksbury Dri. Pen . . . . . . . .3H 11
Hawkshead. Pen . . . . . . . . . .2J 11
Hawkshead Av. Eux . . . . . . . .6B 20
Hawkshead Rd. Rib . . . . . . . . .6E 4
Hawkswood. E'ston . . . . . . . .2D 22
Hawthorn Clo. Ful . . . . . . . . .4F 15
Hawthorn Clo. New L . . . . . . .6E 10
Hawthorn Cres. Lea . . . . . . . .4A 6
Hawthorne Av. High W . . . . . .2J 13
Hawthorne Clo. Clay W . . . . . .3F 17
Hawthorn Rd. Rib . . . . . . . . . .2E 8
            (in two parts)
Hawthorns, The. E'ston . . . . . .1D 22
Hawthorns, The. Ful . . . . . . . .5K 3
Hawthorns, The. Wood . . . . . .1C 2
Haydock Av. Ley . . . . . . . . . .6J 15
Haydocks La. Cot . . . . . . . . . .6B 2
Haydock St. Bam B . . . . . . . .3E 12
Haydock St. Los H . . . . . . . . .6A 12
Hayfield Av. Hogh . . . . . . . . .4K 13
Hayling Pl. Ing . . . . . . . . . . . .7E 2
Haysworth St. Pres . . . . . . . . .2K 7
Haywood Clo. Ful . . . . . . . . . .3A 4
Hazel Av. Bam B . . . . . . . . . .4G 13
Hazel Clo. Bam B . . . . . . . . .4F 13
Hazel Clo. Pen . . . . . . . . . . .2F 11
Hazel Coppice. Lea . . . . . . . . .1C 6
Hazel Gro. Bam B . . . . . . . . .4F 13
Hazel Gro. Chor . . . . . . . . . .4G 21
Hazel Gro. Rib . . . . . . . . . . . .7G 5
Hazelhurst Rd. Rib . . . . . . . . .2G 9
Hazelmere Rd. Ash R . . . . . . .3E 6
Hazelmere Rd. Ful . . . . . . . . .3H 3
Hazels, The. Cop . . . . . . . . . .7C 24
Hazelwood Clo. Ley . . . . . . . .5G 15

Headley Rd. Ley . . . . . . . . . .5G 15
Heald Ho. Rd. Ley . . . . . . . . .7A 16
Heald St. Chor . . . . . . . . . . .7J 21
Healey Vw. Chor . . . . . . . . . .5J 21
Heapey Rd. Chor & H'pey . . . .5K 21
Heather Clo. Chor . . . . . . . . .7J 21
Heather Gro. Rib . . . . . . . . . . .1E 8
Heatherfield Pl. Ash R . . . . . . .3H 7
Heatherleigh. Ley . . . . . . . . .3F 15
Heathers, The. Bam B . . . . . .2G 17
Heatherway. Ful . . . . . . . . . . .6E 4
Heathfield. Hth C . . . . . . . . .7K 25
Heathfield Dri. Rib . . . . . . . . .7E 4
Heathrow Pl. Chor . . . . . . . . .1E 24
Heathway. Ful . . . . . . . . . . . .5K 3
Heatley St. Pres . . . . . . . . . . .5J 7
Heaton Clo. Walt D . . . . . . . . .1D 12
Heaton Mt. Av. Ful . . . . . . . . .4K 3
Heaton Pl. Pres . . . . . . . . . . .3E 8
Heaton St. Ley . . . . . . . . . . .4G 15
Hedgerows Rd. Ley . . . . . . . .6C 14
Hellifield. Ful . . . . . . . . . . . . .4J 3
Helmsley Grn. Ley . . . . . . . . .4K 15
Henderson St. Pres . . . . . . . . .1J 7
            (in two parts)
Hendon Pl. Ash R . . . . . . . . . .2C 6
Hennel Clo. Walt D . . . . . . . . .1C 12
Hennel La. Los H . . . . . . . . . .1C 12
            (in three parts)
Hennel La. Walt D . . . . . . . . .3B 12
Henrietta St. Pres . . . . . . . . . .4B 8
Herbert St. Ley . . . . . . . . . . .5J 15
Herbert St. Pres . . . . . . . . . . .3B 8
Hereford Gro. Cot . . . . . . . . . .6B 2
Hereford Gro. Eux . . . . . . . . .1D 20
Heritage, The. Ley . . . . . . . . .3H 15
Hermon St. Pres . . . . . . . . . . .3C 8
            (in two parts)
Hern Av. Los H . . . . . . . . . . .5A 12
Herschell St. Pres . . . . . . . . . .6A 8
Hesketh Clo. Rib . . . . . . . . . . .3E 8
Hesketh Rd. Rib . . . . . . . . . . .3E 8
Hesketh St. Ash R . . . . . . . . .3G 7
Heversham Av. Ful . . . . . . . . . .4J 3
Hewitt St. Ley . . . . . . . . . . . .4K 15
Hewlett Av. Cop . . . . . . . . . .7B 24
Hewlett St. Cop . . . . . . . . . . .7C 24
Hey End. New L . . . . . . . . . .5D 10
Heyes, The. Clay W . . . . . . . .4F 17
Heysham St. Pres . . . . . . . . . .3J 7
Heys Hunt Av. Ley . . . . . . . . .4J 15
Heys Lodge. Whit W . . . . . . . .1J 21
Heys, The. Cop . . . . . . . . . . .6D 24
Heywood Rd. Ash R . . . . . . . .2C 6
High Bank. H'pey . . . . . . . . . .4K 21
High Cop. Brin . . . . . . . . . . .2K 17
Higher Bank Rd. Ful . . . . . . . .1K 7
Higher Cft. Pen . . . . . . . . . . .3G 11
            (in two parts)
Higher Greenfield. Ing . . . . . . .6F 3
Higher Mdw. Ley . . . . . . . . . .5C 16
Higher Walton Rd.
            Walt D & High W . . . . .7D 8
Highfield. Pres . . . . . . . . . . .3H 11
Highfield Av. Far . . . . . . . . . .3A 16
Highfield Av. Ful . . . . . . . . . . .7C 4
Highfield Av. Los H . . . . . . . .4C 12
Highfield Dri. Ful . . . . . . . . . . .3J 3
Highfield Dri. Pen . . . . . . . . .3H 11
Highfield Gro. Los H . . . . . . . .3C 12
Highfield Ind. Est. Chor . . . . . .5H 21
Highfield Rd. Crost . . . . . . . . .5A 18
Highfield Rd. N. Chor . . . . . . .5G 21
Highfield Rd. S. Chor . . . . . . .6G 21
Highgale Gdns. Los H . . . . . .6C 12
Highgate. Pen . . . . . . . . . . . .7F 7
Highgate Av. Ful . . . . . . . . . . .7J 3
Highgate Clo. Ful . . . . . . . . . .7K 3
High Grn. Ley . . . . . . . . . . . .5H 15
Highgrove Av. Char R . . . . . . .4G 23
Highgrove Ct. Ley . . . . . . . . .5B 14
Highgrove Ho. Chor . . . . . . . .5G 21
Highland Av. Pen . . . . . . . . . .1F 11
Highland Dri. Eux . . . . . . . . .1C 20
High Mdw. Walt D . . . . . . . . .3B 12
Highrigg Dri. Brough . . . . . . . .2K 3
High St. Chor . . . . . . . . . . . .7G 21
High St. Pres . . . . . . . . . . . . .4A 8
Highways Av. Eux . . . . . . . . .6B 20
Hillbrook Grn. Ley . . . . . . . . .4H 15
Hillbrook Rd. Ley . . . . . . . . . .4H 15
Hillcrest Av. Ful . . . . . . . . . . . .3J 3

Hillcrest Av. *Ing* . . . . . . . . . . . . . .7E **2**
Hillcroft. *Ful* . . . . . . . . . . . . . . . .4G **3**
Hillpark Av. *Ful* . . . . . . . . . . . . . .7H **3**
Hillpark Av. *Hogh* . . . . . . . . . . . .4K **13**
Hill Rd. *Ley* . . . . . . . . . . . . . . . . .5A **16**
Hill Rd. *Pen* . . . . . . . . . . . . . . . . .7G **7**
Hill Rd. S. *Pen* . . . . . . . . . . . . . . .2G **11**
Hillside. *Whit W* . . . . . . . . . . . . . .6G **17**
Hillside Av. *Far M* . . . . . . . . . . . .6K **11**
Hillside Av. *Ful* . . . . . . . . . . . . . . .7H **3**
Hillside Clo. *Eux* . . . . . . . . . . . . .6A **20**
Hillside Cres. *Whit W* . . . . . . . . .5G **17**
Hillside Rd. *Pres* . . . . . . . . . . . . .6C **8**
Hills, The. *Pres* . . . . . . . . . . . . . .4H **5**
Hill St. *Pres* . . . . . . . . . . . . . . . . .4K **7**
Hill Top. *New L* . . . . . . . . . . . . . .7E **10**
Hill Top La. *Whit W* . . . . . . . . . . .6G **17**
Hill Vw. Dri. *Cop* . . . . . . . . . . . . .7B **24**
Hill Wlk. *Ley* . . . . . . . . . . . . . . . .4J **15**
Hindley Clo. *Ful* . . . . . . . . . . . . . .4C **4**
Hindley Ho. La. *Ful* . . . . . . . . . . .5C **4**
Hindley St. *Chor* . . . . . . . . . . . . .2F **25**
Hind St. *Pres* . . . . . . . . . . . . . . . .6J **7**
Hodder Av. *Chor* . . . . . . . . . . . . .3F **25**
Hodder Brook. *Rib* . . . . . . . . . . . .1G **9**
Hodder Clo. *Bam B* . . . . . . . . . . .5F **13**
Hodson St. *Bam B* . . . . . . . . . . . .4E **12**
Hogg's La. *Chor* . . . . . . . . . . . . . .3J **25**
Hoghton La.
   *High W & Hogh* . . . . . . . . .2J **13**
Hoghton Rd. *Ley* . . . . . . . . . . . . .5F **15**
Hoghton Vw. *Pres* . . . . . . . . . . . .6C **8**
Holcombe Gro. *Chor* . . . . . . . . . .6J **21**
Holker Clo. *Hogh* . . . . . . . . . . . . .2K **13**
Holker La. *Ley* . . . . . . . . . . . . . . .3B **18**
Holland Av. *Walt D* . . . . . . . . . . . .3E **12**
Holland Ho. Rd. *Walt D* . . . . . . . .2D **12**
Holland Lodge. *Rib* . . . . . . . . . . .7F **5**
   *(off Grange Av.)*
Holland Rd. *Ash R* . . . . . . . . . . . .3G **7**
Hollings. *New L* . . . . . . . . . . . . . .6D **10**
Hollinhead Cres. *Ing* . . . . . . . . . .7F **3**
Hollinhurst Av. *Pen* . . . . . . . . . . .6G **7**
Hollins Gro. *Ful* . . . . . . . . . . . . . .1F **7**
Hollinshead St. *Chor* . . . . . . . . . .7G **21**
Hollins La. *Ley* . . . . . . . . . . . . . . .2E **18**
Hollins Rd. *Pres* . . . . . . . . . . . . . .1B **8**
Hollybank Clo. *Ing* . . . . . . . . . . . .6D **2**
Holly Clo. *Clay W* . . . . . . . . . . . . .4F **17**
Holly Cres. *Cop* . . . . . . . . . . . . . .5C **24**
Holly Pl. *Bam B* . . . . . . . . . . . . . .6H **13**
Hollywood Av. *Pres* . . . . . . . . . . .2G **11**
Holman St. *Pres* . . . . . . . . . . . . . .3C **8**
Holme Rd. *Bam B* . . . . . . . . . . . .5D **12**
Holme Rd. *Pen* . . . . . . . . . . . . . . .5G **7**
Holmes Ct. *Pres* . . . . . . . . . . . . . .1J **7**
Holme Slack La. *Pres* . . . . . . . . . .1B **8**
Holmes Mdw. *Ley* . . . . . . . . . . . .5D **14**
Holmfield Cres. *Lea* . . . . . . . . . . .3B **6**
Holmfield Rd. *Ful* . . . . . . . . . . . . .7A **4**
Holmrook Rd. *Pres* . . . . . . . . . . . .3B **8**
Holsands Clo. *Ful* . . . . . . . . . . . . .5E **4**
Holstein St. *Pres* . . . . . . . . . . . . .4A **8**
Holt Av. *Cop* . . . . . . . . . . . . . . . . .6D **24**
Holt Brow. *Ley* . . . . . . . . . . . . . . .1J **19**
Holt La. *Brin* . . . . . . . . . . . . . . . . .3H **17**
Homestead. *Bam B* . . . . . . . . . . .1F **17**
Homestead Clo. *Ley* . . . . . . . . . .5F **15**
Homestead Farm. *Wstke* . . . . . .6H **11**
Honeysuckle Clo.
   *Whit W* . . . . . . . . . . . . . . . . . .2F **21**
Honeysuckle Row. *Rib* . . . . . . . . .2E **8**
Honiton Way. *Cot* . . . . . . . . . . . . .5D **2**
Hope St. *Chor* . . . . . . . . . . . . . . . .6G **21**
Hope St. *Pres* . . . . . . . . . . . . . . . .4K **7**
Hope Ter. *Los H* . . . . . . . . . . . . . .5A **12**
Hopwood St. *Bam B* . . . . . . . . . . .5E **12**
Hopwood St. *Pres* . . . . . . . . . . . .4A **8**
Horby St. *Pres* . . . . . . . . . . . . . . .4B **8**
Hornbeam Clo. *Pen* . . . . . . . . . . .2F **11**
Hornby Av. *Rib* . . . . . . . . . . . . . . .7E **4**
Hornby Cft. *Ley* . . . . . . . . . . . . . .6D **14**
Hornby Rd. *Chor* . . . . . . . . . . . . .2J **25**
Hornchurch Dri. *Chor* . . . . . . . . . .7E **20**
Hornsea Clo. *Ing* . . . . . . . . . . . . .7E **2**
Hough La. *Ley* . . . . . . . . . . . . . . .5J **15**
Houghton Clo. *Pen* . . . . . . . . . . .2H **11**
Houghton Rd. *Pen* . . . . . . . . . . . .2G **11**
Houghton St. *Chor* . . . . . . . . . . . .7H **21**
Houghton St. *Los H* . . . . . . . . . . .5A **12**
Houldsworth Rd. *Ful* . . . . . . . . . .1J **7**
Howard Rd. *Chor* . . . . . . . . . . . . .3F **25**

Howarth Rd. *Ash R* . . . . . . . . . . . .1H **7**
Howe Gro. *Chor* . . . . . . . . . . . . . .1E **24**
Howgills, The. *Ful* . . . . . . . . . . . . .4A **4**
Howick Cross La. *Pen* . . . . . . . . . .7B **6**
Howick Moor La. *Pen* . . . . . . . . . .2D **10**
Howick Pk. Av. *Pen* . . . . . . . . . . .1D **10**
Howick Pk. Clo. *Pen* . . . . . . . . . .1D **10**
Howick Pk. Dri. *Pen* . . . . . . . . . . .1D **10**
Howick Row. *Pen* . . . . . . . . . . . . .7B **6**
Hoylake Clo. *Ful* . . . . . . . . . . . . . .5F **3**
Hoyles La. *Cot* . . . . . . . . . . . . . . .6A **2**
Hudson Ct. *Bam B* . . . . . . . . . . . .6J **13**
Hudson St. *Pres* . . . . . . . . . . . . . .5A **8**
Hugh Barn La. *New L* . . . . . . . . . .6C **10**
Hugh La. *Ley* . . . . . . . . . . . . . . . .3E **14**
Hull St. *Ash R* . . . . . . . . . . . . . . . .4G **7**
Hunniball Ct. *Ash R* . . . . . . . . . . .2G **7**
Hunstanton Clo. *Eux* . . . . . . . . . .2B **20**
Hunters Lodge. *Walt D* . . . . . . . .2D **12**
Hunters Rd. *Ley* . . . . . . . . . . . . . .5B **16**
Hunters Wood Ct. *Chor* . . . . . . . .2D **24**
Hunts Fld. *Clay W* . . . . . . . . . . . . .4G **17**
Hurst St. *Pres* . . . . . . . . . . . . . . . .4H **7**
Hurn Gro. *Chor* . . . . . . . . . . . . . . .1E **24**
Hurstbrook. *Cop* . . . . . . . . . . . . . .7D **24**
Hurst Pk. *Pen* . . . . . . . . . . . . . . . .1G **11**
Hurstway. *Ful* . . . . . . . . . . . . . . . .4H **3**
Hurstway Clo. *Ful* . . . . . . . . . . . . .4H **3**
Hutton Hall Av. *Hut* . . . . . . . . . . .4C **10**
   *(in two parts)*

**I**

Iddesleigh Rd. *Pres* . . . . . . . . . . .3E **8**
Illingworth Rd. *Pres* . . . . . . . . . . .3E **8**
Ilway. *Walt D* . . . . . . . . . . . . . . . .2D **12**
Ince La. *E'ston* . . . . . . . . . . . . . . . .3E **22**
Ingleborough Way. *Ley* . . . . . . . .4A **16**
Ingle Clo. *Chor* . . . . . . . . . . . . . . .6H **21**
Ingle Head. *Ful* . . . . . . . . . . . . . . .5H **3**
Ingleton Rd. *Rib* . . . . . . . . . . . . . .7E **4**
Ingol Golf Course. . . . . . . . . . . . . .5F **3**
Ingot St. *Pres* . . . . . . . . . . . . . . . .4H **7**
Inkerman St. *Ash R* . . . . . . . . . . . .1G **7**
Inskip Rd. *Ash R* . . . . . . . . . . . . . .3C **6**
Inskip Rd. *Ley* . . . . . . . . . . . . . . . .4F **15**
Intack Rd. *Longt* . . . . . . . . . . . . . .5A **10**
Ipswich Rd. *Rib* . . . . . . . . . . . . . . .2D **8**
Ironside Clo. *Ful* . . . . . . . . . . . . . .7B **4**
Irongate. *Bam B* . . . . . . . . . . . . . .5C **12**
Irvin St. *Pres* . . . . . . . . . . . . . . . . .3B **8**
Isherwood St. *Pres* . . . . . . . . . . . .3C **8**
Isleworth Dri. *Chor* . . . . . . . . . . . .1F **25**
Ivy Bank. *Ful* . . . . . . . . . . . . . . . . .5D **4**
Ivy Clo. *Ley* . . . . . . . . . . . . . . . . . .4C **16**
Ivy Ho. Clo. *Bam B* . . . . . . . . . . . .6H **13**

**J**

Jackson Rd. *Chor* . . . . . . . . . . . . .3E **24**
Jackson Rd. *Ley* . . . . . . . . . . . . . .5F **15**
Jackson St. *Bam B* . . . . . . . . . . . .5F **13**
Jackson St. *Chor* . . . . . . . . . . . . .2H **25**
Jacson St. *Pres* . . . . . . . . . . . . . . .5A **8**
James Pl. *Cop* . . . . . . . . . . . . . . . .7B **24**
James St. *Bam B* . . . . . . . . . . . . .4E **12**
James St. *Pres* . . . . . . . . . . . . . . .5B **8**
Jane La. *Midg H* . . . . . . . . . . . . . .3C **14**
Janice Dri. *Ful* . . . . . . . . . . . . . . . .4H **3**
Jasmine Rd. *Walt D* . . . . . . . . . . .2A **12**
Jeffrey Hill Clo. *Pres* . . . . . . . . . . .4J **5**
Jemmett St. *Pres* . . . . . . . . . . . . .1J **7**
Jeremiah Horrocks Observatory.
   . . . . . . . . . . . . . . . . . . . . . . . . .1K **7**
Jersey Rd. *Eux* . . . . . . . . . . . . . . .1C **20**
Johnspool. *Ful* . . . . . . . . . . . . . . . .5G **3**
John St. *Bam B* . . . . . . . . . . . . . . .4E **12**
John St. *Cop* . . . . . . . . . . . . . . . . .7C **24**
John St. *Ley* . . . . . . . . . . . . . . . . . .5J **15**
Johns Wood Clo. *Chor* . . . . . . . . .2D **24**
John William St. *Pres* . . . . . . . . . .4C **8**
Jordan St. *Pres* . . . . . . . . . . . . . . .5J **7**
Jubilee Av. *Lea* . . . . . . . . . . . . . . .3B **6**
Jubilee Ct. *Ley* . . . . . . . . . . . . . . .6G **15**
Jubilee Pl. *Chor* . . . . . . . . . . . . . .6H **21**
Jubilee Rd. *Los H* . . . . . . . . . . . . .5A **12**
Judd Ho. *Pres* . . . . . . . . . . . . . . . .6J **7**
Judeland. *Chor* . . . . . . . . . . . . . . .5E **20**
Junction Rd. *Ash R* . . . . . . . . . . . .5H **7**
Junction Ter. *Eux* . . . . . . . . . . . . .2A **20**

Juniper Cft. *Clay W* . . . . . . . . . . . .5E **16**
Jutland St. *Pres* . . . . . . . . . . . . . . .4A **8**

**K**

Kane St. *Ash R* . . . . . . . . . . . . . . . .3G **7**
Kaymar Ind. Est. *Pres* . . . . . . . . . .5C **8**
Kay St. *Pres* . . . . . . . . . . . . . . . . . .5J **7**
Keats Clo. *E'ston* . . . . . . . . . . . . . .3F **23**
Keats Way. *Cot* . . . . . . . . . . . . . . .7B **2**
Keepers Wood Clo. *Chor* . . . . . . .2D **24**
Kellet Acre. *Los H* . . . . . . . . . . . . .6A **12**
Kellet Av. *Ley* . . . . . . . . . . . . . . . .5B **16**
Kellet La. *Bam B* . . . . . . . . . . . . . .7H **13**
Kellett St. *Chor* . . . . . . . . . . . . . . .7G **21**
Kem Mill La. *Whit W* . . . . . . . . . . .6F **17**
Kendal Ho. *Pres* . . . . . . . . . . . . . .5A **8**
Kendal St. *Pres* . . . . . . . . . . . . . . .5A **8**
   *(in two parts)*
Kenmure Pl. *Pres* . . . . . . . . . . . . .2K **7**
Kennet Dri. *Ful* . . . . . . . . . . . . . . .3K **3**
Kennett Dri. *Ley* . . . . . . . . . . . . . .4K **15**
Kennington Rd. *Ful* . . . . . . . . . . . .7A **4**
Kennington Av. *Pen* . . . . . . . . . . .6F **7**
Kennington Rd. *Chor* . . . . . . . . . .1F **25**
Kent Av. *Walt D* . . . . . . . . . . . . . . .2D **12**
Kent Dri. *Ley* . . . . . . . . . . . . . . . . .4B **16**
Kent St. *Pres* . . . . . . . . . . . . . . . . .2K **7**
Kenyon La. *H'pey* . . . . . . . . . . . . .7K **17**
Kerr Pl. *Pres* . . . . . . . . . . . . . . . . . .4H **7**
Kershaw St. *Chor* . . . . . . . . . . . . .6J **21**
Kew Gdns. *Far* . . . . . . . . . . . . . . . .3K **15**
Kew Gdns. *Pen* . . . . . . . . . . . . . . .7F **7**
Kidlington Clo. *Los H* . . . . . . . . . .5C **12**
Kidsgrove. *Ing* . . . . . . . . . . . . . . . .6D **2**
Kilkerran Clo. *Chor* . . . . . . . . . . . .7H **21**
Kilmuir Clo. *Ful* . . . . . . . . . . . . . . .6C **4**
Kilncroft. *Clay W* . . . . . . . . . . . . . .3F **17**
Kilngate. *Los H* . . . . . . . . . . . . . . .2C **12**
Kilruddery Rd. *Pres* . . . . . . . . . . .7J **7**
Kilsby Clo. *Walt D* . . . . . . . . . . . . .2E **12**
Kilshaw St. *Pres* . . . . . . . . . . . . . .4K **7**
Kimberley Rd. *Ash R* . . . . . . . . . . .2G **7**
Kimberley St. *Cop* . . . . . . . . . . . . .7C **24**
Kingfisher Clo. *Chor* . . . . . . . . . . .3D **24**
Kingfisher St. *Pres* . . . . . . . . . . . .2B **8**
Kingfisher Way. *Bam B* . . . . . . . . .3G **13**
Kingsbarn Clo. *Ful* . . . . . . . . . . . . .5D **4**
Kingsbridge Clo. *Pen* . . . . . . . . . .4J **11**
Kings Ct. *Ley* . . . . . . . . . . . . . . . . .5J **15**
Kings Cres. *Ley* . . . . . . . . . . . . . . .5J **15**
King's Cft. *Walt D* . . . . . . . . . . . . .7D **8**
King's Cft. M. *Walt D* . . . . . . . . . .7D **8**
Kingsdale Av. *Rib* . . . . . . . . . . . . .6D **4**
Kingsdale Clo. *Ley* . . . . . . . . . . . .1K **19**
Kingsdale Clo. *Walt D* . . . . . . . . .7F **9**
Kings Dri. *Ful* . . . . . . . . . . . . . . . . .6H **3**
Kingsfold Dri. *Pen* . . . . . . . . . . . . .3G **11**
Kingshaven Dri. *Pen* . . . . . . . . . . .3J **11**
Kings Lea. *Adl* . . . . . . . . . . . . . . . .7K **25**
Kingsley Dri. *Chor* . . . . . . . . . . . . .3E **24**
Kingsley Rd. *Cot* . . . . . . . . . . . . . .5C **2**
Kingsmead. *Chor* . . . . . . . . . . . . .3G **25**
Kingsmuir Av. *Ful* . . . . . . . . . . . . .7D **4**
King St. *Chor* . . . . . . . . . . . . . . . . .2H **25**
King St. *Ley* . . . . . . . . . . . . . . . . . .5J **15**
King St. *Los H* . . . . . . . . . . . . . . . .6B **12**
Kingsway. *Ash R* . . . . . . . . . . . . . .2D **6**
Kingsway. *Bam B* . . . . . . . . . . . . .5E **12**
Kingsway. *Eux* . . . . . . . . . . . . . . . .5C **20**
Kingsway. *Ley* . . . . . . . . . . . . . . . .7G **15**
Kingsway. *Pen* . . . . . . . . . . . . . . . .6F **7**
Kingsway W. *Brough* . . . . . . . . . . .1G **3**
Kingsway W. *Pen* . . . . . . . . . . . . . .6E **6**
Kingswood Rd. *Ley* . . . . . . . . . . . .5J **15**
Kingswood St. *Pres* . . . . . . . . . . . .5J **7**
Kirkby Av. *Ley* . . . . . . . . . . . . . . . .5C **16**
Kirkham Clo. *Ley* . . . . . . . . . . . . . .5F **15**
Kirkham St. *Pres* . . . . . . . . . . . . . .4J **7**
Kirkland Pl. *Ash R* . . . . . . . . . . . . .4C **6**
Kirkstall Clo. *Chor* . . . . . . . . . . . . .3H **25**
Kirkstall Dri. *Chor* . . . . . . . . . . . . .3H **25**
Kirkstall Rd. *Chor* . . . . . . . . . . . . .3H **25**
Kittlingbourne Brow.
   *High W* . . . . . . . . . . . . . . . . . .2G **13**
Knebworth Clo. *Clay W* . . . . . . . .4G **17**
Knot Acre. *New L* . . . . . . . . . . . . . .5E **10**
Knot La. *Walt D* . . . . . . . . . . . . . . .7E **8**

Knowles St. *Chor* . . . . . . . . . . . . . .2G **25**
Knowles St. *Pres* . . . . . . . . . . . . . .4D **8**
Knowles Wood Dri. *Chor* . . . . . . .2E **24**
Knowley Brow. *Chor* . . . . . . . . . . .5J **21**
Knowsley Av. *Far* . . . . . . . . . . . . . .2A **16**
Knowsley Rd. *Ley* . . . . . . . . . . . . .6A **16**
Knowsley St. *Pres* . . . . . . . . . . . . .5A **8**
   *(in two parts)*
Korea Rd. *Ful* . . . . . . . . . . . . . . . . .6B **4**

**L**

Laburnum Av. *Los H* . . . . . . . . . . .5B **12**
Laburnum Clo. *Pres* . . . . . . . . . . .1C **8**
Laburnum Dri. *Ful* . . . . . . . . . . . . .3H **3**
Laburnum Rd. *Chor* . . . . . . . . . . . .4G **21**
Lacy Av. *Pen* . . . . . . . . . . . . . . . . .3J **11**
Lady Bank Av. *Ful* . . . . . . . . . . . . .4D **4**
Lady Crosse Dri. *Whit W* . . . . . . .7G **17**
Lady Hey Cres. *Lea* . . . . . . . . . . . .3A **6**
Ladyman St. *Pres* . . . . . . . . . . . . .5J **7**
Lady Pl. *Walt D* . . . . . . . . . . . . . . .1E **12**
Ladysmith Rd. *Ash R* . . . . . . . . . .2G **7**
Lady St. *Pres* . . . . . . . . . . . . . . . . .4K **7**
Ladyway Dri. *Ful* . . . . . . . . . . . . . .4C **4**
Ladywell St. *Pres* . . . . . . . . . . . . . .4J **7**
Lakeland Gdns. *Chor* . . . . . . . . . .3E **24**
Lambert Clo. *Rib* . . . . . . . . . . . . . .1E **8**
Lambert Rd. *Rib* . . . . . . . . . . . . . .1D **8**
Lancashire Dri. *Ley* . . . . . . . . . . . .2J **15**
Lancashire Enterprise Bus. Pk.
   *Ley* . . . . . . . . . . . . . . . . . . . . .2J **15**
*Lancashire Lynx R.L.F.C.* . . .2H **25**
   *(off Duke St., Victory Pk.)*
Lancaster Av. *Ley* . . . . . . . . . . . . .5C **16**
Lancaster Ct. *Chor* . . . . . . . . . . . . .5G **21**
Lancastergate. *Ley* . . . . . . . . . . . .6H **15**
Lancaster Ho. *Ley* . . . . . . . . . . . . .3J **15**
Lancaster Ho. *Pres* . . . . . . . . . . . .5A **8**
Lancaster La. *Ley* . . . . . . . . . . . . .5B **16**
Lancaster Rd. *Pres* . . . . . . . . . . . .4K **7**
Lancaster Rd. N. *Pres* . . . . . . . . . .3K **7**
Lancaster St. *Cop* . . . . . . . . . . . . .7D **24**
Lancaster Way. *Pres* . . . . . . . . . . .4A **8**
   *(off St John's Shop. Cen.)*
Land La. *Longt* . . . . . . . . . . . . . . . .7B **10**
Landseer St. *Pres* . . . . . . . . . . . . .3C **8**
Lane Ends Trad. Est. *Ash R* . . . . .1G **7**
Langcliffe Rd. *Rib* . . . . . . . . . . . . .7E **4**
Langdale Clo. *Walt D* . . . . . . . . . .4D **12**
Langdale Ct. *Pen* . . . . . . . . . . . . . .1G **11**
Langdale Cres. *Rib* . . . . . . . . . . . .1E **8**
Langdale Gro. *Whit W* . . . . . . . . .7F **17**
Langdale Rd. *Ley* . . . . . . . . . . . . . .1J **19**
Langdale Rd. *Rib* . . . . . . . . . . . . . .1E **8**
Langden Cres. *Bam B* . . . . . . . . . .6F **13**
Langden Dri. *Rib* . . . . . . . . . . . . . .1G **9**
Langden Fold. *Grims* . . . . . . . . . .2K **5**
Langfield Clo. *Ful* . . . . . . . . . . . . . .3K **3**
Langholme Clo. *Ley* . . . . . . . . . . .6F **15**
Langholme Rd. *Pen* . . . . . . . . . . .1E **10**
Langport Clo. *Ful* . . . . . . . . . . . . . .3K **3**
Langton Brow. *E'ston* . . . . . . . . . .3E **22**
Langton Clo. *E'ston* . . . . . . . . . . . .3F **23**
Langton Clo. *Ley* . . . . . . . . . . . . . .6E **14**
Langton St. *Pres* . . . . . . . . . . . . . .5H **7**
Lansborough Clo. *Ley* . . . . . . . . . .6C **14**
Lansdown Hill. *Ful* . . . . . . . . . . . . .3G **3**
Lappet Gro. *Cot* . . . . . . . . . . . . . . .6C **2**
Larch Av. *Chor* . . . . . . . . . . . . . . . .5J **21**
Larches Av. *Ash R* . . . . . . . . . . . . .3D **6**
Larches La. *Ash R* . . . . . . . . . . . . .3C **6**
Larch Ga. *Ful* . . . . . . . . . . . . . . . . .4C **4**
Larch Ga. *Hogh* . . . . . . . . . . . . . . .3K **13**
Larch Gro. *Bam B* . . . . . . . . . . . . .4F **13**
Larchwood. *Ash R* . . . . . . . . . . . . .3C **6**
Larchwood. *Pen* . . . . . . . . . . . . . . .1F **11**
Larchwood Cres. *Ley* . . . . . . . . . .5G **15**
Lark Av. *Pen* . . . . . . . . . . . . . . . . . .1J **11**
Larkfield. *E'ston* . . . . . . . . . . . . . . .2D **22**
Lark Hill. *High W* . . . . . . . . . . . . . . .2H **13**
Larkhill Rd. *Pres* . . . . . . . . . . . . . .5B **8**
Larkhill St. *Pres* . . . . . . . . . . . . . . .5B **8**
Latham St. *Pres* . . . . . . . . . . . . . . .6A **8**
Latimer Dri. *Ley* . . . . . . . . . . . . . . .5D **10**
Lauderdale Cres. *Rib* . . . . . . . . . .7F **5**
Lauderdale Rd. *Rib* . . . . . . . . . . . .7F **5**
Lauderdale St. *Pres* . . . . . . . . . . . .6J **7**
Laund, The. *Ley* . . . . . . . . . . . . . . .5C **14**
Laurel Av. *Eux* . . . . . . . . . . . . . . . .4K **19**
Laurel Bank Av. *Ful* . . . . . . . . . . . .1G **7**

Laurels, The. *Cop* ....6D 24
Laurel St. *Pres* ....5A 8
Lavender Clo. *Ful* ....5C 4
Lavender Gro. *Chor* ....3G 25
Lawnwood Av. *Chor* ....3E 24
Lawrence Av. *Pres* ....7B 8
Lawrence Av. *Walt D* ....3D 12
Lawrence La. *E'ston* ....1E 22
Lawrence Rd. *Chor* ....1F 25
Lawrence Rd. *Pen* ....7F 7
Lawrence St. *Ful* ....1H 7
Lawson St. *Chor* ....7J 21
Lawson St. *Pres* ....4K 7
Laxey Gro. *Pres* ....1D 8
Layton Rd. *Ash R* ....3C 6
Leach Pl. *Bam B* ....5H 13
Leadale. *Lea* ....2B 6
Leadale Grn. *Ley* ....5F 15
Leadale Rd. *Ley* ....5F 15
Leafy Clo. *Ley* ....7K 15
Leagram Cres. *Rib* ....1F 9
Lea Rd. *Cot & Lea T* ....7A 2
Lea Rd. *Whit W* ....2G 21
Leek St. *Pres* ....4E 8
Leesands Clo. *Ful* ....6D 4
Leeson Av. *Char R* ....4B 24
 (in two parts)
Leeward La. *Ash R* ....4D 6
Leicester Lodge. *Rib* ....7F 5
 (off Grange Av.)
Leicester Rd. *Pres* ....3A 8
Leigh Brow. *Bam B* ....3B 12
Leigh Row. *Chor* ....1G 25
Leigh St. *Chor* ....1G 25
Leighton St. *Pres* ....4J 7
Lennon St. *Chor* ....1G 25
Lennox St. *Pres* ....5A 8
Leo Case Ct. *Pres* ....4D 8
Letchworth Dri. *Chor* ....2F 25
Letchworth Pl. *Chor* ....2F 25
Levens Dri. *Ley* ....4B 16
Levensgarth Av. *Ful* ....3K 3
Levens St. *Pres* ....3D 8
Lever Ho. La. *Ley* ....4A 16
Lex St. *Pres* ....4C 8
Leyburn Clo. *Rib* ....6E 4
Leyfield. *Pen* ....3H 11
Leyfield Rd. *Ley* ....5H 15
Leyland Golf Course. ....6B 16
Leyland La. *Ley* ....5E 18
Leyland Rd. *Pen & Los H* ....7H 7
Leyland Way. *Ley* ....5K 15
Leyton Av. *Ley* ....7F 15
Leyton Grn. *Ley* ....7G 15
Library Rd. *Clay W* ....2F 17
Library St. *Chor* ....1G 25
Library St. *Pres* ....5A 8
Lichen Clo. *Char R* ....4B 24
Lichfield Rd. *Ash R* ....2D 6
Lichfield Rd. *Chor* ....5A 8
Lidget Av. *Lea* ....3A 6
Liege Rd. *Ley* ....6J 15
Lightfoot Clo. *Ful* ....3H 3
Lightfoot Grn. La. *L Grn* ....3F 3
Lightfoot La. *High B & Ful* ....4D 2
 (in three parts)
Lighthurst Av. *Chor* ....2G 25
Lighthurst La. *Chor* ....3H 25
Lilac Av. *Pen* ....3K 11
Lilac Gro. *Pres* ....1C 8
Lily Gro. *Pres* ....1C 8
Limbrick Rd. *Chor* ....1J 25
Lime Chase. *Ful* ....3G 3
Lime Clo. *Pen* ....1E 10
Lime Gro. *Ash R* ....2D 6
Lime Gro. *Chor* ....3G 25
Limes Av. *Eux* ....3A 20
Limes, The. *Pres* ....3B 8
Lincoln Chase. *Lea* ....3A 6
Lincoln Ho. *Pres* ....5B 8
 (off Arundel Pl.)
Lincoln St. *Pres* ....3B 8
Lincoln Wlk. *Pres* ....3B 8
Lindale Av. *Grims* ....2K 5
Lindale Rd. *Ful* ....7A 4
Linden Clo. *Los H* ....4B 12
Linden Dri. *Los H* ....5B 12
Linden Gro. *Chor* ....4H 21
Linden Gro. *Rib* ....1E 8
Lindle Av. *Hut* ....3C 10
Lindle Clo. *Hut* ....3C 10
Lindle Cres. *Hut* ....3C 10

Lindle La. *Hut* ....2C 10
Lindley St. *Los H* ....5A 12
Lindsay Av. *Ley* ....5K 15
Lindsay Dri. *Chor* ....1E 24
Lingwell Clo. *Whit W* ....2G 21
Linksfield. *Ful* ....1G 7
Links Ga. *Ful* ....1G 7
Links Rd. *Pen* ....6F 7
Linnet St. *Pres* ....2B 8
Linton Gro. *Pen* ....7E 6
Linton St. *Ful* ....1H 7
Liptrott Rd. *Chor* ....3E 24
Lit. Banks Clo. *Bam B* ....7H 13
Lit. Carr La. *Chor* ....3H 25
Little Clo. *Far M* ....3G 15
Little Clo. *Pen* ....2G 11
Lit. Wood Clo. *Chor* ....2D 24
Liverpool Rd. *Hut & Pen* ....4A 10
Livesey St. *Pres* ....5B 8
Lockhart Rd. *Pres* ....2K 7
Lockside Rd. *Ash R* ....5D 6
Lodge Clo. *Bam B* ....4F 13
Lodge La. *Far M* ....6H 11
Lodge St. *Pres* ....4H 7
 (in two parts)
Lodge Vw. *Far M* ....6J 11
Lodge Vw. *Pen* ....2K 11
Lodge Wood Clo. *Chor* ....2E 24
Lodgings, The. *Ful* ....5C 4
Lomond Clo. *Eux* ....3B 20
London Rd. *Pres* ....4B 8
London Way. *Walt D* ....1C 12
Long Acre. *Bam B* ....1G 17
Longbrook Av. *Bam B* ....3E 12
Long Butts. *Pen* ....3H 11
Long Clo. *Ley* ....6C 14
Long Copse. *Chor* ....6D 20
Long Cft. Mdw. *Chor* ....4F 21
Longfield. *Ful* ....3J 3
Longfield. *Pen* ....7F 7
Longfield Av. *Cop* ....6C 24
Longfield Mnr. *Chor* ....3E 24
Long La. *Hth C* ....3K 25
Longley Clo. *Ful* ....3K 3
Long Mdw. *Chor* ....3E 24
Longmeanygate.
 *Midg H & Ley* ....4C 14
Long Moss. *Ley* ....6C 14
Long Moss La.
 *New L & Wstke* ....7C 10
Longridge Rd. *Rib & Grims* ....7F 5
Longsands La. *Ful* ....6C 4
Longton By-Pass.
 *L Hoo & Longt* ....7A 10
Longton St. *Chor* ....7J 21
Longworth Av. *Cop* ....6D 24
 (in two parts)
Longworth St. *Bam B* ....3E 12
Longworth St. *Chor* ....2F 25
Longworth St. *Pres* ....3C 8
Lonmore. *Walt D* ....2D 12
Lonsdale Chase. *Los H* ....5A 12
Lonsdale Clo. *Ley* ....1J 19
Lonsdale Rd. *Pres* ....3C 8
Lord Nelson Wharf. *Ash R* ....4F 7
Lord's Av. *Los H* ....6B 12
Lords Cft. *Clay W* ....4E 16
Lord's La. *Pen* ....4J 11
Lord St. *Chor* ....1H 25
Lord St. *E'ston* ....3E 22
Lord St. *Pres* ....4A 8
Lord St. *Whit W* ....5G 17
Lord's Wlk. *Pres* ....4A 8
Lorraine Av. *Ful* ....1J 7
Lorton Clo. *Ful* ....5K 3
Lostock Ct. *Los H* ....6B 12
Lostock La.
 *Los H & Bam B* ....6C 12
Lostock Mdw. *Clay W* ....5E 16
Lostock Sq. *Los H* ....6B 12
Lostock Vw. *Los H* ....6A 12
Lourdes Av. *Los H* ....4A 12
Lovat Rd. *Pres* ....2K 7
Low Cft. *Wood* ....1F 3
Lwr. Bank Rd. *Ful* ....1K 7
Lwr. Burgh Way. *Chor* ....4E 24
Lwr. Copthurst La.
 *Whit W* ....7J 17
Lwr. Croft. *Pen* ....3H 11
Lwr. Field. *Far M* ....7K 11
Lwr. Greenfield. *Ing* ....7F 3

Lwr. Hill Dri. *Hth C* ....7K 25
Lwr. House Rd. *Ley* ....6G 15
Lowesby Clo. *Walt D* ....2E 12
Low Grn. *Ley* ....5H 15
Lowick Clo. *Hogh* ....1K 13
Lowndes St. *Pres* ....2J 7
 (in two parts)
Lowood Gro. *Lea* ....3B 6
Lowry Clo. *Los H* ....6A 12
Lowther Cres. *Ley* ....3F 15
Lowther Dri. *Ley* ....4F 15
Lowther St. *Ash R* ....3G 7
Lowthian Ho. *Pres* ....4K 7
 (off Lowthian St.)
Lowthian St. *Pres* ....4K 7
Lowthorpe Cres. *Pres* ....2B 8
Lowthorpe Pl. *Pres* ....2B 8
Lowthorpe Rd. *Pres* ....1B 8
Loxley Gro. *Ful* ....5C 4
Loxwood Clo. *Walt D* ....2A 12
Lucas Av. *Chor* ....4B 8
Lucas Dri. *Whit W* ....1G 21
Lucas La. *Whit W* ....2G 21
Lucas La. E. *Whit W* ....2G 21
Lucerne Clo. *Ful* ....7C 4
Lucerne Rd. *Ful* ....7C 4
Lulworth Av. *Ash R* ....2H 7
Lulworth Pl. *Walt D* ....3D 12
Lulworth Rd. *Ful* ....7A 4
Lund St. *Pres* ....4K 7
Lune Dri. *Ley* ....4C 16
Lune St. *Pres* ....5K 7
Lupin Clo. *Whit W* ....2F 21
Lupton St. *Chor* ....1G 25
Luton Rd. *Ash R* ....2C 6
Lutwidge Av. *Pres* ....3C 8
Lychfield Dri. *Bam B* ....6E 12
Lychgate. *Pres* ....4A 8
Lydd Gro. *Chor* ....1E 24
Lydgate. *Chor* ....3E 24
Lydiate La. *E'ston* ....7D 18
Lydiate La. *Ley* ....2A 16
Lydric Av. *Hogh* ....5K 13
Lyndale Av. *Los H* ....3C 12
Lyndale Clo. *Ley* ....1K 19
Lyndale Gro. *Los H* ....3C 12
Lyndeth Clo. *Ful* ....5E 4
Lynethurst Dri. *Ash R* ....2C 6
Lynn Pl. *Rib* ....2D 8
Lynton Av. *Ley* ....6A 16
Lynwood Av. *Grims* ....1J 5
Lyons La. *Chor* ....1H 25
Lytham Clo. *Ful* ....1H 7
Lytham Rd. *Ash R* ....1G 7
Lytham St. *Chor* ....1J 25
Lytham St. *Ful* ....7G 3

# M

Mackay Cft. *Chor* ....7H 21
McKenna M. *Pen* ....7F 7
Mackenzie Clo. *Chor* ....7H 21
McKenzie St. *Bam B* ....5F 13
Maddy St. *Pres* ....4H 7
Mafeking Rd. *Ash R* ....2G 7
Magnolia Clo. *Ful* ....5C 4
Magnolia Dri. *Ley* ....4C 16
Magnolia Rd. *Pen* ....2F 11
Main Sprit Weind. *Pres* ....5A 8
Mainway Ct. *Bam B* ....5E 12
Maitland Clo. *Pres* ....4C 8
Maitland St. *Pres* ....4C 8
 (in two parts)
Malcolm St. *Pres* ....3D 8
Malden St. *Ley* ....5J 15
Maldon Pl. *Rib* ....2D 8
Malham Pl. *Rib* ....2D 8
Mallard Clo. *Ley* ....6F 15
Mallards Wlk. *Bam B* ....1E 16
Mallom Av. *Eux* ....6C 20
Mallowdale. *Ful* ....5F 3
Mall, The. *Rib* ....2E 8
Malthouse Ct. *Ash R* ....3H 7
Malthouse, The. *Ash R* ....3H 7
Malthouse Way. *Pen* ....2H 11
Maltings, The. *Pen* ....1H 25
Malton Dri. *Los H* ....6A 12
Malvern Av. *Pres* ....7B 8
Malvern Clo. *Los H* ....5C 12
Malvern Ho. *Pen* ....3J 11

Malvern Rd. *Pres* ....6B 8
Manchester Mill Ind. Est.
 *Pres* ....4C 8
Manchester Rd. *Pres* ....5A 8
Manning Rd. *Pres* ....3E 8
 (in two parts)
Manor Av. *Ful* ....7B 4
Manor Av. *Pen* ....1F 11
Manor Clo. *Ful* ....4F 3
Manor Ct. *Ful* ....4F 3
Manor Gro. *Pen* ....1E 10
Manor Ho. Clo. *Ley* ....6D 14
Manor Ho. Cres. *Pres* ....1B 8
Manor Ho. La. *Pres* ....1B 8
Manor La. *Pen* ....1E 10
Manor Pk. *Ful* ....1C 8
Manor Rd. *Clay W* ....3F 17
Manston Gro. *Chor* ....1E 24
Maplebank. *Lea* ....3A 6
Maple Cres. *Pres* ....5J 7
Maple Dri. *Bam B* ....4F 13
Maple Gro. *Chor* ....4H 21
Maple Gro. *Grims* ....2K 5
Maple Gro. *Pen* ....1F 11
Maple Gro. *Rib* ....7G 5
Maple Ho. *Chor* ....2D 24
Maples, The. *Ley* ....1B 18
Maplewood Clo. *Chor* ....2J 25
Maplewood Clo. *Ley* ....6G 15
Marathon Pl. *Ley* ....3E 14
Mardale Cres. *Ley* ....7K 15
Mardale Rd. *Pres* ....3G 9
Maresfield Rd. *Pres* ....7H 7
Margaret Rd. *Pen* ....1J 11
Margaret St. *Pres* ....4A 8
Margate Rd. *Ing* ....7E 2
Marilyn Av. *Los H* ....5B 12
Marina Clo. *Los H* ....4A 12
Marina Dri. *Ful* ....4J 3
Marina Dri. *Los H* ....4A 12
Marina Gro. *Los H & Pen* ....4A 12
Marine Cres. *Eux* ....1D 20
Mariners Way. *Ash R* ....4E 6
Maritime Way. *Ash R* ....5D 6
Mark Clo. *Pen* ....4K 11
Market Pl. *Chor* ....7G 21
Market Pl. *Pres* ....5K 7
Market Sq. *Pres* ....4K 7
Market St. *Chor* ....7G 21
Market St. W. *Pres* ....4K 7
Market Wlk. *Chor* ....7G 21
Markham St. *Ash R* ....3G 7
Markland St. *Pres* ....5J 7
Mark's Av. *Far M* ....1G 15
Marl Av. *Pen* ....1F 11
Marlborough Dri. *Ful* ....4H 3
Marlborough Dri. *Walt D* ....1D 12
Marlborough St. *Chor* ....6J 21
Marl Cft. *Pen* ....3H 11
Marlfield Clo. *Ing* ....6D 2
Marl Hill Cres. *Rib* ....2G 9
Marron Clo. *Ley* ....6G 15
Marsden Clo. *E'ston* ....1D 22
Marsett Pl. *Rib* ....6E 4
Marshall Gro. *Ing* ....7E 2
Marshall Ho. *Pres* ....4K 7
 (off Ring Way)
Marshall's Brow. *Pen* ....2J 11
Marshall's Clo. *Pen* ....1J 11
Marsh La. *Brin* ....3K 17
Marsh La. *Pres* ....5H 7
Marsh Way. *Pen* ....3G 11
Marston Clo. *Ful* ....4G 3
Marston Moor. *Ful* ....4G 3
Martindales, The. *Clay W* ....3E 16
Martinfield. *Ful* ....3K 3
Martinfield Rd. *Pen* ....3H 11
Martins Av. *Hth C* ....6J 25
Marton Rd. *Ash R* ....4D 6
Marybank Clo. *Ful* ....5C 4
Masefield Pl. *Walt D* ....3D 12
Masonfield. *Bam B* ....1F 17
Mason Hill Vw. *Ful* ....7A 4
Mason Ho. Cres. *Ing* ....6E 2
Mason St. *Pres* ....5J 21
Masonwood. *Ful* ....5A 4
Matlock Pl. *Ing* ....6E 2
Matterdale Rd. *Ley* ....7K 15
Maudland Bank. *Pres* ....4J 7
Maudland Rd. *Pres* ....4J 7
Maud St. *Chor* ....2F 25
Maureen Av. *Los H* ....5B 12
Mavis Dri. *Cop* ....7C 24

Mayfield Av. Ing .........6E 2
(in two parts)
Mayfield Av. Los H .......5C 12
Mayfield Rd. Ash R ........3F 7
Mayfield Rd. Chor ........6H 21
Mayfield Rd. Ley .........7J 15
Mayflower Av. Pen ......2E 10
Maynard St. Ash R .......2H 7
Maypark. Bam B ........1E 16
Mead Av. Ley ..........6K 15
Meadow Bank. Bam B ....2F 17
Meadow Bank. Pen ......2G 11
Meadowbarn Clo. Cot ....6C 2
Meadow Ct. Pres ........6J 7
Meadowcroft. Eux ......4K 19
Meadowcroft Rd. Ley ....7F 15
Meadowfield. Ful ........3K 3
Meadowfield. Pen .......3J 11
Meadowland Clo. Far M ..3G 15
Meadowlands. Char R ....4B 24
Meadow La. Bam B ......2F 17
Meadow Reach. Pen ......2F 11
Meadowside Dri. Hogh ...4K 13
Meadows, The. Hesk ....6G 23
Meadow St. Ley .........5J 15
Meadow St. Pres .........4A 8
Meadow St. Wheel ......7K 17
Meadow, The. Ley .......5D 14
Meadow Va. Ley ........6C 14
Meadow Vw. Hth C .....7K 25
Meadow Way. Cop .......7B 24
Meads Rd. Ash R ........3F 7
Meadway. Clay W ........3F 17
Meadway. Pen ..........7E 6
Mealhouse La. Chor .....7G 21
Meanygate. Bam B ......5E 12
Mearley Rd. Rib .........7E 4
Meath Rd. Pres ..........6H 7
Medway. Ful ...........5K 3
Medway Clo. Los H .....4B 12
Medway Ho. Pres ........4D 8
(off Leo Case Ct.)
Melba Rd. Rib ..........1E 8
Melbert Av. Ful .........1G 7
Melbourne St. Pres .......4K 7
Melford Clo. Chor ......4J 21
Mellia Dri. Ley .........4C 16
Mellings Fold. Pres ......6C 8
Melling St. Pres .........4K 7
Mellor Pl. Pres ..........5B 8
Mellor Rd. Ley .........4F 15
Melrose Av. Ful .........6B 4
Melrose Way. Chor ......2H 25
Melton Pl. Ley .........5K 15
Menai Dri. Ful ..........4H 3
Mendip Rd. Ley ........5B 16
Mercer Ct. Hth C .......7K 25
Mercer Rd. Los H ......4A 12
Mercer St. Pres .........4C 8
Mere Clo. Brough ........1G 3
Merefield. Chor ........6E 20
Mere Fold. Char R ......5B 24
Merlin Gro. Ley ........6E 14
Merrick Av. Pres ........4F 9
Merryburn Clo. Ful ......7A 4
Merry Trees La. Cot .....6B 2
Mersey St. Ash R ........4G 7
Merton Av. Ful .........5K 3
Merton Gro. Chor ......4K 21
Mete St. Pres ..........4D 8
Methuen Av. Ful .........5J 3
Mickleden Av. Ful ......4K 3
Middlefield. Ley ........6C 14
Middleforth Grn. Pen ....1J 11
Middlewood Clo. E'ston ..2E 22
Midge Hall La. Midg H ...1A 14
Midgery Ct. Ful .........4C 4
Midgery La. Brough & Ful .2A 4
(in two parts)
Miles St. Pres ..........2K 7
Mile Stone Mdw. Eux ...3B 20
Miles Wlk. Pres .........2J 7
Millbank. Ful ..........1G 7
Millbank. Pres ..........4B 8
Millbrook Clo. Wheel ....7K 17
Millbrook Way. Pen ......3F 11
Millcombe Way. Walt D ..2E 12
Millcroft. Chor ........5E 20
Mill Cct. Ash R .........2G 7
(off Atherton Clo.)
Mill Cft. Ful ...........7G 3
Miller Arc. Pres .........5A 8

Miller Fld. Lea .........1C 6
Millergate. Cot .........7C 2
Miller La. Cot .........5C 2
Miller Rd. Pres & Rib ....3D 8
Miller's La. Ley .......3D 14
Miller St. Pres .........4C 8
Millfield Rd. Chor ......6F 21
Miller St. Pres .........3K 7
Millgate. Eux .........7B 20
Mill Ga. Ful ...........1H 7
Millhaven. Ful .........7H 3
Mill Hill. Pres .........4J 7
Mill La. Char R .......6J 23
Mill La. Clay W & Whit W .5G 17
Mill La. Cop ..........7C 24
Mill La. E'ston ........3E 22
Mill La. Eux ..........6J 19
(in two parts)
Mill La. Far M .........3G 15
Mill La. Ley ...........7G 3
Mill La. Ley ..........6F 15
Mill La. Walt D .........7D 8
Mill Row. Pen .........2K 11
Millstone Clo. Cop ......7D 24
Mill St. Cop ...........7C 24
Mill St. Far ...........3K 15
Mill St. Ley ..........6F 15
Mill St. Pres ..........4H 7
Mill St. Wheel ........7K 17
Mill St. Ley ..........4F 15
Millwood Glade. Chor ...6F 21
Millwood Rd. Los H .....2B 12
Milner St. Pres .........2K 7
Milton Clo. Walt D ......3D 12
Milton Rd. Cop ........7C 24
Milton Ter. Chor .......5H 21
Mimosa Clo. Chor ......4E 20
Mimosa Rd. Rib .........2E 8
Minster Pk. Cot .........6C 2
Mitton Dri. Rib ........1G 9
Moira Cres. Rib .........7E 4
Molyneux Ct. Pres ......4A 8
Mona Pl. Pres ..........4J 7
Monks Wlk. Pen .........6G 7
Montcliffe Rd. Chor ....6J 21
Montgomery St. Bam B ...5F 13
Montjoly St. Pres .......5C 8
Montrose Clo. Chor .....2J 25
Moody La. Maw ........7A 22
Moon St. Bam B ........5E 12
Moor Av. Pen ..........2D 10
Moorbrook St. Pres ......3J 7
Moorcroft. Brough ......1F 3
Moorcroft Cres. Rib .....1D 8
Moore St. Pres ..........5C 8
Moor Fld. New L ......6E 10
Moorfield Clo. Ful .......3J 3
Moorfield Dri. Rib .......1E 8
Moorfield Rd. Ley ......6E 14
Moorfields. Chor .......6J 21
Moorfields Av. Ful .......3J 3
Moorgate. Ful .........6K 3
Moor Hall St. Pres .......2J 7
Moorhey Cres. Bam B ...5G 13
Moorhey Cres. Pen .......7F 7
Moorhey Dri. Pen .......7F 7
Moorings, The. Chor ....7J 21
Moorland Av. Rib ........6D 4
Moorland Cres. Rib ......6D 4
Moorland Ga. Chor .....2K 25
Moorlands. Pres .........1J 7
Moor La. Hut .........4B 10
Moor La. Pres ..........4K 7
Moor Pk. Av. Pres .......2K 7
Moor Rd. Chor ........3E 24
Moor Rd. Crost ........4A 18
Moorside Av. Rib ........1F 9
Moorside Dri. Pen ......2F 11
Morland Av. Los H .....6A 12
Morley Cft. Far M ......3G 15
Mornington Rd. Pen ......7F 7
Mornington Rd. Pres .....3F 9
Morris Clo. Ley ........6J 15
Morris Ct. Rib ..........2D 8
Morris Cres. Rib .........2D 8
Morris Rd. Chor .......6J 21
Morris Rd. Rib ..........2D 8
Mosley St. Ley .........5J 15
Mosley St. Pres .........4C 8

Moss Acre Rd. Pen .....2J 11
Moss Av. Ash R .........2E 6
(in two parts)
Moss Bank. Cop ........7C 24
Moss Bri. Pk. Los H ....5C 12
Mossbrook Dri. Cot ......6D 2
Moss Clo. Chor ........7J 21
Moss Clo. Chor ........7D 4
Mossfield Clo. Los H ....5B 12
Mossfield Rd. Chor .....7J 21
Moss Ho. Rd. Wood .....1F 3
Mosslands. Ley .........5F 15
Moss La. Breth ........6A 14
Moss La. Cop ..........7C 24
Moss La. Far M ........1E 14
(in two parts)
Moss La. Ley ..........4K 15
(Station Brow)
Moss La. Ley ..........1B 18
(Willow Rd.)
Moss La. Los H ........5B 12
Moss La. New L ........5B 10
Moss La. Pen ..........5J 11
Moss La. Whit W .......2G 21
Moss Side Ind. Est. Ley ..6D 14
Moss Side Way. Ley .....7D 14
Moss St. Los H ........5B 12
Moss St. Pen ..........4J 7
Moss Ter. Whit W .......2J 21
Mossway. New L ........7D 10
Moss Wood Clo. Chor ...2E 24
Mottram Clo. Whit W ...2G 21
Mounsey Rd. Bam B .....5F 13
Mountain Rd. Cop ......7C 24
Mountbatten Rd. Chor ...2F 25
Mt. Pleasant. Pres ......4K 7
Mt. Pleasant. Whit W ...6G 17
Mount St. Pres .........5K 7
Muirfield. Pen ..........6E 6
Muirfield Clo. Eux ......3B 20
Muirfield Clo. Ful .......5F 3
Mulberry Av. Pen ......2E 10
Mulgrave Av. Ash R .....3E 6
Muncaster Rd. Pres .....2K 7
Munro Cres. Rib .........1E 8
Murdock Av. Ash R ......2H 7
Murray Av. Far M ......1G 15
Murray St. Ley .........5K 15
Murray St. Pres .........3J 7
Museum of Lancashire. ..4B 8
Mythop Pl. Ash R ........3D 6

## N

Nab Rd. Chor ..........6J 21
Nab Wood Dri. Chor .....2E 24
Naptha La. Wstke ......6J 21
(in two parts)
Nares St. Ash R .........3G 7
Narrow La. Midg H ......4B 14
Nateby Pl. Ash R ........3D 6
National Football Mus. ...2B 8
Navigation Bus. Cen. Ash R .4D 6
Navigation Way. Ash R ...4D 6
Neapsands Clo. Ful ......6D 4
Neare Mdw. Brin .......3G 17
Neargates. Char R ......5B 24
Neath Clo. Walt D ......2E 12
Nell La. Ley ..........2B 16
Nelson Av. Ley .........5K 15
Nelson Cres. Lea ........2B 6
Nelson Dri. Lea ........2B 6
Nelson Rd. Chor .......1G 25
Nelson St. Bam B .......5E 12
Nelson St. Pres .........4H 7
Nelson Way. Ash R ......5C 6
Nene Clo. Ley .........7K 15
Neston St. Pres .........4E 8
Netherley Rd. Cop ......7C 24
Nevett St. Pres .........4D 8
Newark Pl. Ash R ........2C 6
Newark Pl. Ful .........3H 3
New Brook Ho. Pres .....4C 8
Newbury Clo. Ful ........3G 3
Newbury Grn. Ful ........3G 3
Newby Dri. Ley .........4B 16
Newby Pl. Rib ..........3G 3
(in two parts)
Newcock Yd. Pres .......5K 7
Newfield Rd. Bam B .....6G 13
Newgate. Ful ...........7J 3

Newgate La. Wstke ......5G 11
New Hall La. Pres ........4B 8
Newlands. E'ston .......2E 22
Newlands Rd. Pen .......1E 10
New La. E'ston .........5C 18
New La. Pen ...........2J 11
New Links Av. Ing .......5E 2
Newlyn Pl. Ing ..........6D 2
New Mkt. St. Chor ......7G 21
New Mill St. E'ston .....2E 22
New Moss La. Whit W ...2G 21
New Pastures. Los H ....5C 12
New Rd. Cop ..........6D 24
New Rd. Los H .........4B 12
New Rough Hey. Ing .....5D 2
Newsham Hall La. Wood ...1D 2
Newsham St. Ash R .......3H 7
Newsome St. Ley ........5J 15
New St. E'ston .........2E 22
Newton Av. Pres .........4G 9
Newton Clo. Ley .......6D 14
Newton Ct. Ash R ........3F 7
Newton Rd. Ash R ........2F 7
Newton St. Pres .........4A 8
(in two parts)
Nib La. Pen ...........5J 11
Nichol St. Chor ........6G 21
Nightingale Way. Chor ...3D 24
Nile Clo. Ash R .........4D 6
Nimes St. Pres ..........4D 8
Nine Elms. Ful .........5G 3
Nixon Ct. Ley ..........6B 14
Nixon La. Ley ..........6B 14
Noel Sq. Rib ...........3E 8
Nook Cres. Grims .......2J 5
Nookfield. Ley .........5C 14
Nook Glade. Grims .......2J 5
Nooklands. Ful .........7J 3
Nook La. Bam B ........6D 12
Nook La. Maw .........3A 22
Noor St. Pres ..........3A 8
Norbreck Dri. Ash R .....3C 6
Norcross Pl. Ash R .......3D 6
Norfolk Clo. Ley .......7G 15
Norfolk Rd. Pres .........3A 8
Norfolk Rd. Walt D .....1D 12
Normandy Rd. Wood .....1F 3
Norris St. Chor ........2G 25
Norris St. Ful & Pres .....1H 7
(in two parts)
Northbrook Gdns. Ley ...5G 15
Northbrook Rd. Ley .....4G 15
(in two parts)
N. Cliff St. Pres ........6J 7
Northcote Rd. Pres ......5H 7
Northcote St. Ley ......5J 15
Northenden Rd. Cop .....7C 24
Northgate. Ley .........4K 15
Northgate Dri. Chor .....5J 21
North Gro. Los H .......5C 12
N. Highfield. Ful ........5E 4
Northlands. Ful .........5J 3
Northlands. Ley ........7E 14
Northleach Av. Pres .....3K 11
N. Ribble St. Walt D .....6C 8
North Rd. Pres .........3K 7
Northside. Eux .........4A 20
North St. Chor ........5G 21
North St. Pres ..........4K 7
N. Syke Av. Lea .........3A 6
Northumberland Ho. Pres .4K 7
Northumberland St. Chor .1H 25
North Va. Hth C .......7K 25
Northway. Brough .......1G 3
Northway. Ful ..........5H 3
Norwich Pl. Pres .........5A 8
Nottingham Rd. Pres .....3A 8
Nursery Clo. Char R .....4C 24
Nursery Clo. Ley .......6H 15
Nursery La. New L ......5C 10
Nutter Rd. Pres .........5J 7

## O

Oak Av. Eux ..........4B 20
Oak Av. Pen ...........2F 11
Oak Cft. Clay W .......4F 17
Oak Dri. Ley ..........4G 21
Oakengate. Ful .........4C 4
Oakenhead St. Pres .....3E 8
Oakfield. Ash R .........3F 7

Oakfield. Ful . . . . . . . . . . .4K 3
Oakfield Dri. Ley . . . . . . . . . .6D 14
Oak Gro. New L . . . . . . . . . . .7E 10
Oakham Ct. Pres . . . . . . . . . . .5A 8
Oak Ho. Chor . . . . . . . . . . . .2D 24
Oakland Glen. Walt D . . . . . . . .2A 12
Oaklands Dri. Pen . . . . . . . . . .1E 10
Oaklands Gro. Ash R . . . . . . . . .3C 6
Oakland St. Bam B . . . . . . . . . .4E 12
Oakmere. Brin . . . . . . . . . . . .3G 17
Oakridge Clo. Ful . . . . . . . . . .4K 3
Oakshott Pl. Bam B . . . . . . . . .6H 13
Oaks, The. Chor . . . . . . . . . . .4F 25
Oaks, The. Walt D . . . . . . . . . .2B 12
Oak St. Pres . . . . . . . . . . . . .5A 8
Oaktree Av. Ing . . . . . . . . . . .7E 2
Oak Tree Av. Ley . . . . . . . . . . .2B 16
Oaktree Clo. Ing . . . . . . . . . . .7E 2
Oak Vw. Ley . . . . . . . . . . . . .4G 15
Oakwood Av. Walt D . . . . . . . . .1C 12
Oakwood Dri. Ful . . . . . . . . . . .3H 3
Oakwood Rd. Chor . . . . . . . . . .2F 25
Oakwood Rd. Cop . . . . . . . . . .6D 24
Oakwood Vw. Chor . . . . . . . . . .4F 25
Oakworth Av. Rib . . . . . . . . . . .6F 5
Oban Ct. Grims . . . . . . . . . . . .2K 5
Oban Cres. Pres . . . . . . . . . . .1D 8
Odell Way. Walt D . . . . . . . . . .2E 12
Old Bri. Way. Chor . . . . . . . . . .6H 21
Old Brown La. Bam B . . . . . . . . .2G 13
Oldcock Yd. Pres . . . . . . . . . . .5A 8
Old Cft. Ful . . . . . . . . . . . . .3H 3
Old Dawber's La. Eux . . . . . . . . .6K 19
Oldfield. Pen . . . . . . . . . . . .3H 11
Oldfield Rd. Bam B . . . . . . . . . .6G 13
Old Greaves Town La.
  Lea . . . . . . . . . . . . . . . .3B 6
Old Hall Clo. Bam B . . . . . . . . .5E 12
Old Hall Dri. Bam B . . . . . . . . .5E 12
Old Hall La. Char R . . . . . . . . .2K 23
Old Hey Cft. Pen . . . . . . . . . . .3H 11
Old Lancaster La. Pres . . . . . . . .3H 7
Old Millstones. Pres . . . . . . . . .5H 7
Old Mill Ter. Chor . . . . . . . . . .6J 21
Old Oak Gdns. Walt D . . . . . . . .2B 12
Old Pope La. Wstke . . . . . . . . . .5F 11
Old School Clo. Ley . . . . . . . . .6C 14
Old School La. Eux . . . . . . . . . .4B 20
  (in two parts)
Old School La. Los H . . . . . . . . .7C 12
Old Station Clo. Grims . . . . . . . .2K 5
Old Tram Rd. Bam B . . . . . . . . .5E 12
  (in two parts)
Old Tram Rd.
  Pen & Walt D . . . . . . . . . . .1A 12
  (in three parts)
Old Vicarage. Pres . . . . . . . . . .4A 8
Olive Clo. Whit W . . . . . . . . . .2G 21
Olivers Pl. Ful . . . . . . . . . . . .3A 4
Orchard Av. New L . . . . . . . . . .6E 10
Orchard Clo. Eux . . . . . . . . . . .3B 20
Orchard Clo. Ing . . . . . . . . . . .6E 2
Orchard Cft. Los H . . . . . . . . . .5A 12
Orchard St. Ley . . . . . . . . . . .5K 15
Orchard St. Pres . . . . . . . . . . .4K 7
Orchard, The. Wood . . . . . . . . .2C 2
Orchard Wlk. Grims . . . . . . . . . .1J 5
Ord Rd. Ash R . . . . . . . . . . . .2G 7
Ormskirk Rd. Pres . . . . . . . . . .4A 8
Orrell Clo. Ley . . . . . . . . . . . .5F 15
Orrest Rd. Pres . . . . . . . . . . . .3G 9
Osborne Dri. Clay W . . . . . . . . .4G 17
Osborne Rd. Walt D . . . . . . . . . .2D 12
Osborne St. Pres . . . . . . . . . . .5J 7
Osprey Pl. Ley . . . . . . . . . . . .4E 14
Oswald Rd. Ash R . . . . . . . . . . .3G 7
Otters Clo. Rib . . . . . . . . . . . .2F 9
Otway St. Pres . . . . . . . . . . . .2J 7
Outgate. Cot . . . . . . . . . . . . .7B 2
Outram Way. Bam B . . . . . . . . . .5E 12
Overton Rd. Ash R . . . . . . . . . .4C 6
Owens St. Chor . . . . . . . . . . . .1J 25
Owen St. Pres . . . . . . . . . . . .4B 8
Owtram St. Pres . . . . . . . . . . .4C 8
Oxford M. Eux . . . . . . . . . . . .1C 20
Oxford Rd. Bam B . . . . . . . . . . .5F 13
Oxford Rd. Ful . . . . . . . . . . . .7H 3
Oxford St. Chor . . . . . . . . . . . .1G 25
Oxford St. Pres . . . . . . . . . . . .5A 8
Ox Hey Av. Lea . . . . . . . . . . . .2A 6
Oxheys Ind. Est. Pres . . . . . . . .2H 7

Oxheys St. Pres . . . . . . . . . . .2H 7
Oxley Rd. Pres . . . . . . . . . . . .3D 8
  (in two parts)

## P

Paddock Av. Ley . . . . . . . . . . .6C 14
Paddock, The. Ful . . . . . . . . . . .5A 4
Paddock, The. Pen . . . . . . . . . .3J 11
Padway. Pen . . . . . . . . . . . . .3H 11
Pages Ct. Los H . . . . . . . . . . .6B 12
Paley Rd. Pres . . . . . . . . . . . .5H 7
Pall Mall. Chor . . . . . . . . . . . .2G 25
Paradise Clo. Whit W . . . . . . . . .6F 17
Paradise La. Ley . . . . . . . . . . .5D 14
Paradise St. Chor . . . . . . . . . . .4K 21
Parish Gdns. Ley . . . . . . . . . . .4J 15
Park Av. Eux . . . . . . . . . . . . .5B 20
Park Av. New L . . . . . . . . . . . .4C 10
Park Av. Pres . . . . . . . . . . . . .2B 8
Park Clo. Pen . . . . . . . . . . . . .7H 7
Park Clo. Rib . . . . . . . . . . . . .1D 8
Park Dri. Lea . . . . . . . . . . . . .3B 6
Parker La. Pen . . . . . . . . . . . .2J 11
  (in two parts)
Parker St. Ash R . . . . . . . . . . .2H 7
Parker St. Chor . . . . . . . . . . . .6G 21
Parkers Wood Clo. Chor . . . . . . .2E 24
Parkfield Av. Ash R . . . . . . . . . .2F 7
Parkfield Clo. Lea . . . . . . . . . . .3A 6
Parkfield Clo. Ley . . . . . . . . . . .6E 14
Parkfield Cres. Lea . . . . . . . . . .4A 6
Parkfield Dri. Lea . . . . . . . . . . .4A 6
Parkfield Vw. Lea . . . . . . . . . . .4A 6
Parkgate Dri. Ley . . . . . . . . . . .7G 15
Pk. Hall Rd. Char R & Hesk . . .4G 23
Parklands Av. Pen . . . . . . . . . . .1E 10
Parklands Clo. Pen . . . . . . . . . .1E 10
Parklands Dri. Ful . . . . . . . . . . .3J 3
Parklands Gro. Ful . . . . . . . . . . .3J 3
Parkgate Dri. Ley . . . . . . . . . . .7G 15
Pk. Mill Pl. Pres . . . . . . . . . . . .3A 8
Park Pl. Pres . . . . . . . . . . . . .5K 7
  (off Glovers Ct.)
Park Pl. Walt D . . . . . . . . . . . .1E 12
Park Rd. Chor . . . . . . . . . . . . .6G 21
Park Rd. Cop . . . . . . . . . . . . .7C 24
Park Rd. Ful . . . . . . . . . . . . . .7A 4
Park Rd. Ley . . . . . . . . . . . . . .7J 15
Park Rd. Pres . . . . . . . . . . . . .4A 8
  (in two parts)
Parkside. Lea . . . . . . . . . . . . .2B 6
Parkside. Pres . . . . . . . . . . . . .1B 8
Parkside Av. Chor . . . . . . . . . . .7G 21
Parkside Dri. Whit W . . . . . . . . .1F 21
Parkside Dri. S. Whit W . . . . . . . .1F 21
Park St. Chor . . . . . . . . . . . . .6G 21
Park St. E'ston . . . . . . . . . . . .2E 22
Parkthorn Rd. Lea . . . . . . . . . . .4A 6
Park Vw. H'pey . . . . . . . . . . . .4K 21
Park Vw. Pres . . . . . . . . . . . . .1H 11
Pk. View Av. Pen . . . . . . . . . . .2F 7
Park Wlk. Ful . . . . . . . . . . . . .1A 8
Park Way. Pen . . . . . . . . . . . . .1H 11
Park Way Cvn. Site. Pen . . . . . . .1H 11
Parlick Rd. Ful . . . . . . . . . . . .2G 9
Parr Cottage Clo. E'ston . . . .1E 22
Parr La. E'ston . . . . . . . . . . . .1E 22
Parrock Clo. Pen . . . . . . . . . . .2J 11
Parsons Brow. Chor . . . . . . . . . .1G 25
Pasture Fld. Clo. Ley . . . . . . . . .5E 14
Pastures, The. Grims . . . . . . . . .2J 5
Patten St. Pres . . . . . . . . . . . .4K 7
Pavilions, The. Ash R . . . . . . . . .5G 7
Peachtree Clo. Ful . . . . . . . . . . .5D 4
Peacock Hall Rd. Ley . . . . . . . . .7F 15
Peacockhill Clo. Pres . . . . . . . . .4H 5
Pear Tree Av. Cop . . . . . . . . . . .5C 24
Pear Tree Clo. Walt D . . . . . . . . .3E 12
Pear Tree Cres. Walt D . . . . . . . .3E 12
Pear Tree La. Eux . . . . . . . . . . .4C 20
Pear Tree Rd. Clay W . . . . . . . . .3B 8
Pear Tree St. Bam B . . . . . . . . .3E 12
Pechell St. Ash R . . . . . . . . . . .3G 7
Pedder's Gro. Ash R . . . . . . . . .4E 6
Pedder's La. Ash R . . . . . . . . . .4E 6
Pedder St. Ash R . . . . . . . . . . .4H 7
Pedder's Way. Ash R . . . . . . . . .4E 6
Peel Hall St. Pres . . . . . . . . . . .3B 8
Peel St. Ash R . . . . . . . . . . . .4J 7

Peel St. Chor . . . . . . . . . . . . .1G 25
Pembroke Pl. Chor . . . . . . . . . .2F 25
Pembroke Pl. Ley . . . . . . . . . . .6J 15
Pembury Av. Pen . . . . . . . . . . .2K 11
Pendle Hill Clo. Pres . . . . . . . . .4J 5
Pendle Rd. Ley . . . . . . . . . . . .5B 16
Penguin St. Pres . . . . . . . . . . .3G 9
Pennine Av. Eux . . . . . . . . . . . .6B 20
Pennine Rd. Chor . . . . . . . . . . .7J 21
Pennines, The. Ful . . . . . . . . . . .4A 4
Penny St. Pres . . . . . . . . . . . . .4A 8
Penwortham Ct. Pen . . . . . . . . .1H 11
Penwortham Golf Course. . . . .5F 7
Penwortham Hall Gdns.
  Pen . . . . . . . . . . . . . . . .2J 11
Penwortham Way. Pres . . . . . . . .3F 11
Penwortham Way. Wstke . . . . . .4G 11
Pen-y-Ghent Way. Ley . . . . . . . .4A 16
Percy St. Chor . . . . . . . . . . . .1H 25
Percy St. Pres . . . . . . . . . . . . .4A 8
Peregrine Pl. Ley . . . . . . . . . . .4F 15
Perthshire Gro. Eux . . . . . . . . . .1C 20
Peterfield Rd. Pen . . . . . . . . . . .3H 11
Petersan Ct. Chor . . . . . . . . . . .4G 21
Peter St. Chor . . . . . . . . . . . . .7G 21
Petunia Clo. Ley . . . . . . . . . . .4C 16
Pickerings, The. Los H . . . . . . . .5C 12
Pikestone Ct. Chor . . . . . . . . . .1J 25
Pilling Clo. Chor . . . . . . . . . . . .2H 25
Pilling La. Chor . . . . . . . . . . . .3G 25
Pincock Brow. Eux . . . . . . . . . . .7A 20
Pincock St. Eux . . . . . . . . . . . .6A 20
Pine Clo. Rib . . . . . . . . . . . . . .7F 5
Pine Gro. Chor . . . . . . . . . . . . .4H 21
Pines Clo. Bam B . . . . . . . . . . .2G 17
Pines, The. Ley . . . . . . . . . . . .6B 14
Pine Walks. Lea . . . . . . . . . . . .3A 6
Pineway. Ful . . . . . . . . . . . . . .7G 3
Pinewood Cres. Ley . . . . . . . . . .6G 15
Pinewood Rd. Pen . . . . . . . . . . .3A 12
Pinfold Clo. Ful . . . . . . . . . . . .6E 4
Pinfold St. Pres . . . . . . . . . . . .4D 8
Pingle Cft. Clay W . . . . . . . . . . .4E 16
Pintail Clo. Ley . . . . . . . . . . . .4A 16
Pippin St. Brin . . . . . . . . . . . .2J 17
Pitman Ct. Ful . . . . . . . . . . . . .3B 4
Pitman Way. Ful . . . . . . . . . . . .3B 4
  (in two parts)
Pitt St. Pres . . . . . . . . . . . . . .5J 7
Plant St. Ash R . . . . . . . . . . . .3G 7
Pleasant Vw. Cop . . . . . . . . . . .6D 24
Plevna Rd. Pres . . . . . . . . . . . .4C 8
Plock Grn. Chor . . . . . . . . . . . .3G 25
Ploughlands, The. Ash R . . . . . . .3C 6
Plover St. Pres . . . . . . . . . . . . .2B 8
Plumpton Fld. Wood . . . . . . . . . .1C 2
Plumpton Rd. Ash R . . . . . . . . . .2G 7
Plumtree Clo. Ful . . . . . . . . . . . .5C 4
Plungington Rd. Ful & Pres . . .1H 7
Plymouth Gro. Chor . . . . . . . . . .7J 21
Polefield. Ful . . . . . . . . . . . . . .4J 3
Pole St. Pres . . . . . . . . . . . . . .4A 8
Pollard St. Pres . . . . . . . . . . . .4J 7
Poole Rd. Ful . . . . . . . . . . . . . .7A 4
Pool Ho Ct. Ing . . . . . . . . . . . .5E 2
Pool Ho. La. Ing . . . . . . . . . . . .6D 2
Pope La. Rib . . . . . . . . . . . . . .2F 9
Pope La. Wstke & Pen . . . . . . . .6F 11
Pope Wlk. Pen . . . . . . . . . . . . .2H 11
Poplar Av. Bam B . . . . . . . . . . .4F 13
Poplar Av. Eux . . . . . . . . . . . . .3A 20
Poplar Clo. Bam B . . . . . . . . . . .4F 13
Poplar Dri. Cop . . . . . . . . . . . .7D 24
Poplar Dri. Pen . . . . . . . . . . . .7G 7
Poplar Gro. Bam B . . . . . . . . . .4F 13
Poplar Gro. Rib . . . . . . . . . . . .7G 5
Poplar St. Chor . . . . . . . . . . . .2H 25
Poppy Av. Chor . . . . . . . . . . . .5H 21
Poppyfield. Cot . . . . . . . . . . . .5D 2
Porter Pl. Pres . . . . . . . . . . . . .6A 8
Porter St. Pres . . . . . . . . . . . . .3B 8
Portland St. Chor . . . . . . . . . . .7H 21
Portland St. Pres . . . . . . . . . . .5H 7
Portman St. Pres . . . . . . . . . . . .3B 8
Portree Clo. Ful . . . . . . . . . . . .6C 4
Portsmouth Dri. Chor . . . . . . . . .7J 21
Port Way. Ash R . . . . . . . . . . . .4G 7
Potter La. High W . . . . . . . . . . .6J 9
Potter La. Sam . . . . . . . . . . . .3K 9
Poulton Cres. Hogh . . . . . . . . . .2K 13
Poulton St. Ash R . . . . . . . . . . .3G 7
Powis Rd. Ash R . . . . . . . . . . .4E 6

Poynter St. Pres . . . . . . . . . . . .3C 8
Preesall Clo. Ash R . . . . . . . . . .3C 6
Preesall Rd. Ash R . . . . . . . . . . .3C 6
Preston Ent. Cen. Pres . . . . . . . .3K 7
Preston Golf Course. . . . . . . .5B 4
Preston Grasshoppers R.U.F.C.
  . . . . . . . . . . . . . . . . . .3F 3
  (Lightfoot Grn. La.)
Preston New Rd.
  Sam & Mel B . . . . . . . . . .3H 9
  (in two parts)
Preston Nook. E'ston . . . . . . . . .3E 22
Preston North End F.C. . . . . . . .2B 8
  (Deepdale)
Preston Rd.
  Bam B & Clay W . . . . . . . .7G 13
Preston Rd. Char R . . . . . . . . . .5K 23
Preston Rd. Cop & Stand . . .7A 24
Preston Rd. Grims . . . . . . . . . . .3J 5
Preston Rd. Ley . . . . . . . . . . . .4K 15
Preston Sports Arena. . . . . . . .1B 6
Preston St. Chor . . . . . . . . . . . .5G 21
Preston Technology Cen.
  Pres . . . . . . . . . . . . . . . .4H 7
Pretoria St. Bam B . . . . . . . . . .5E 12
Primrose Gro. Pres . . . . . . . . . .1C 8
Primrose Hill. Pres . . . . . . . . . . .5B 8
Primrose Hill Rd. Eux . . . . . . . . .4K 19
Primrose La. Pres . . . . . . . . . . .1C 8
Primrose Rd. Pres . . . . . . . . . . .1C 8
Primrose St. Chor . . . . . . . . . . .7H 21
Princes Ct. Pen . . . . . . . . . . . .6F 7
Princes Dri. Ful . . . . . . . . . . . .5J 3
Princes Reach. Ash R . . . . . . . . .4E 6
Princes Rd. Pen . . . . . . . . . . . .6F 7
Prince's Rd. Walt D . . . . . . . . . .7E 8
Princess St. Bam B . . . . . . . . . .5F 13
Princess St. Chor . . . . . . . . . . .2H 25
Princess St. Ley . . . . . . . . . . . .5K 15
Princess St. Los H . . . . . . . . . . .6B 12
Princess St. Pres . . . . . . . . . . .5B 8
Princess Way. Eux . . . . . . . . . . .5B 20
Pringle Wood. Brough . . . . . . . . .1G 3
Prior's Oak Cotts. Pen . . . . . . . . .7G 7
Priory Clo. Ley . . . . . . . . . . . . .4A 16
Priory Clo. Pen . . . . . . . . . . . . .6G 7
Priory Cres. Pen . . . . . . . . . . . .6G 7
Priory La. Pen . . . . . . . . . . . . .7F 7
Priory St. Ash R . . . . . . . . . . . .4H 7
Progress St. Chor . . . . . . . . . . .7J 21
Prospect Av. Los H . . . . . . . . . .5B 12
Prospect Pl. Ash R . . . . . . . . . . .3F 7
Prospect Pl. Pen . . . . . . . . . . . .1J 11
Prospect Vw. Los H . . . . . . . . . .6B 12
Pump Ho. La. Ley . . . . . . . . . . .1B 18
Pump St. Pres . . . . . . . . . . . . .4A 8

## Q

Quarry Rd. Chor . . . . . . . . . . . .2J 25
Queens Ct. Ful . . . . . . . . . . . . .1J 7
  (off Queens Rd.)
Queenscourt Av. Pen . . . . . . . . .3J 11
Queensdale Clo. Walt D . . . . . . .1E 12
Queen's Dri. Ful . . . . . . . . . . . .5H 3
Queensgate. Chor . . . . . . . . . . .1F 25
Queen's Gro. Chor . . . . . . . . . . .7G 21
Queen's Lancashire
  Regiment Mus. . . . . . . . . .7B 4
  (off Watling St. Rd.)
Queens Retail Pk. Pres . . . . . . . .5B 8
Queen's Rd. Chor . . . . . . . . . . .7F 21
Queens Rd. Ful . . . . . . . . . . . .1H 7
Queen's Rd. Walt D . . . . . . . . . .7E 8
Queen St. Los H . . . . . . . . . . . .6B 12
Queen St. Pres . . . . . . . . . . . . .5B 8
Queen St. E. Chor . . . . . . . . . . .2H 25
Queensway. Ash R . . . . . . . . . . .2D 6
Queensway. Bam B . . . . . . . . . .4E 12
Queensway. Eux . . . . . . . . . . . .5C 20
Queensway. Ley . . . . . . . . . . . .7G 15
Queensway. Pen . . . . . . . . . . . .6F 7
Queensway. Clo. Pen . . . . . . . . . .6F 7
Quins Cft. Ley . . . . . . . . . . . . .4J 15
Quin St. Ley . . . . . . . . . . . . . .5J 15

## R

Radburn Brow. Clay W . . . . . . . .3F 17
Radburn Clo. Clay W . . . . . . . . .3F 17

Radnor St. *Pres* . . . . . . . . . . .4J 7
Raglan Rd. *Ash R* . . . . . . . . . .2H 7
(off Raglan St.)
Raglan St. *Ash R* . . . . . . . . . .2H 7
Raikes Rd. *Pres* . . . . . . . . . . .3C 8
Railway Rd. *Chor* . . . . . . . . .6H 21
Railway St. *Chor* . . . . . . . . . .1H 25
Railway St. *Ley* . . . . . . . . . . .4K 15
Railway Ter. *Cop* . . . . . . . . . .7D 24
Raleigh Rd. *Ful* . . . . . . . . . . . .5J 3
Ramsey Av. *Pres* . . . . . . . . . . .1D 8
Ranaldsway. *Ley* . . . . . . . . . .6F 15
Ranglet Rd. *Bam B* . . . . . . . .6H 13
Rangletts Av. *Chor* . . . . . . . .2G 25
Ranglit Av. *Lea* . . . . . . . . . . . .3A 6
Ratten La. *Hut* . . . . . . . . . . .2A 10
Raven Clo. *Chor* . . . . . . . . . .3D 24
Ravenhill Dri. *Chor* . . . . . . . .6G 21
Ravensthorpe. *Chor* . . . . . . .6E 20
Raven St. *Pres* . . . . . . . . . . . .2C 8
Ravenswood. *Rib* . . . . . . . . . . .2E 8
Rawcliffe Av. *Ash R* . . . . . . . . .4C 6
Rawcliffe Rd. *Chor* . . . . . . . .1G 25
Rawlinson La. *Hth C* . . . . . . . .6J 25
Rawstorne Rd. *Pen* . . . . . . . . .7F 7
Rectory Clo. *Chor* . . . . . . . . .7G 21
Red Bank. *Chor* . . . . . . . . . . .3H 25
Redcar Av. *Ley* . . . . . . . . . . . .7D 2
Red Cross St. *Pres* . . . . . . . . . .5J 7
Redhill. *Hut* . . . . . . . . . . . . .4A 10
Redhill Gro. *Chor* . . . . . . . . .4J 21
Red Ho. La. *E'ston* . . . . . . . . .2D 22
Red La. *E'ston* . . . . . . . . . . . .1F 23
Redmayne St. *Pres* . . . . . . . . .4D 8
Red Rose Dri. *Ley* . . . . . . . . .2H 15
Redsands Dri. *Ful* . . . . . . . . . .6D 4
Red Scar Ind. Est. *Rib* . . . . . . .6G 5
(in two parts)
Redwing Dri. *Chor* . . . . . . . . .3D 24
Redwood Av. *Ley* . . . . . . . . . .5G 15
Redwood Dri. *Chor* . . . . . . . .2H 25
Reedfield. *Bam B* . . . . . . . . . .2G 17
Reedfield Pl. *Bam B* . . . . . . . .7F 13
Reeveswood. *E'ston* . . . . . . . .2D 22
Regency Av. *Los H* . . . . . . . .6D 12
Regent Ct. *Ful* . . . . . . . . . . . . .6J 3
Regent Dri. *Ful* . . . . . . . . . . . .7H 3
Regent Gro. *Ful* . . . . . . . . . . . .6J 3
Regent Pk. *Ful* . . . . . . . . . . . . .5J 3
Regent Rd. *Chor* . . . . . . . . . .1F 25
Regent Rd. *Ley* . . . . . . . . . . .5H 15
Regent Rd. *Walt D* . . . . . . . .1D 12
Regent St. *Cop* . . . . . . . . . . .7C 24
Regent St. *Pres* . . . . . . . . . . . .6K 7
Regentsway. *Bam B* . . . . . . . .4E 12
Regents Way. *Eux* . . . . . . . . .5B 20
Reigate. *Chor* . . . . . . . . . . . .4K 21
Reiver Rd. *Ley* . . . . . . . . . . . .3E 14
Renshaw Dri. *Walt D* . . . . . . .3E 12
Rhoden Rd. *Ley* . . . . . . . . . . .5E 14
Rhodesway. *Hogh* . . . . . . . . .3K 13
Ribble Bank. *Pen* . . . . . . . . . . .6F 7
Ribble Bank St. *Pres* . . . . . . . .5J 7
Ribble Brook Ho. *Pres* . . . . . . .3J 7
Ribble Clo. *Pen* . . . . . . . . . . .1J 11
Ribble Clo. *Pres* . . . . . . . . . . .6J 7
Ribble Ct. *Ash R* . . . . . . . . . . .3G 7
Ribble Ct. *Pres* . . . . . . . . . . . .6H 7
Ribble Cres. *Walt D* . . . . . . . . .6C 8
Ribble Hall. *Pres* . . . . . . . . . . .3K 7
(off Ashmoor St.)
Ribble Ho. *Pres* . . . . . . . . . . .4D 8
(off Cliffe Ct.)
Ribble Rd. *Ley* . . . . . . . . . . . .6F 15
Ribblesdale Dri. *Grims* . . . . . . .3J 5
Ribblesdale Pl. *Chor* . . . . . . . .1F 25
Ribblesdale Pl. *Pres* . . . . . . . . .6K 7
Ribble St. *Pres* . . . . . . . . . . . .5J 7
Ribbleton Av. *Pres & Rib* . . . . .3D 8
Ribbleton Hall Cres. *Rib* . . . . . .1F 9
Ribbleton Hall Dri. *Rib* . . . . . . .1F 9
Ribbleton La. *Pres* . . . . . . . . . .4B 8
Ribbleton Pl. *Pres* . . . . . . . . . .4B 8
Ribbleton St. *Pres* . . . . . . . . . .4B 8
Ribby Pl. *Ash R* . . . . . . . . . . . .3D 6
Richmond Ct. *Ley* . . . . . . . . .5D 14
Richmond Ho. *Pres* . . . . . . . . .5A 8
(off Pembroke Pl.)
Richmond Rd. *Chor* . . . . . . . .2J 25
Richmond Rd. *E'ston* . . . . . . .1E 22
Richmond St. *Pres* . . . . . . . . . .5B 8
Ridgeford Gdns. *Ful* . . . . . . . .6H 3

Ridgemont. *Ful* . . . . . . . . . . . .5G 3
Ridge Rd. *Chor* . . . . . . . . . . .1J 25
Ridgeway. *Pen* . . . . . . . . . . .1J 11
Ridings, The. *Whit W* . . . . . . .1G 21
Riding St. *Pres* . . . . . . . . . . . .3K 7
Ridley La. *Maw* . . . . . . . . . . .6A 22
Ridley Rd. *Ash R* . . . . . . . . . . .2G 7
Rigby St. *Pres* . . . . . . . . . . . . .3C 8
Riley Clo. *Ley* . . . . . . . . . . . .6J 15
Ringway. *Chor* . . . . . . . . . . . .1E 24
Ring Way. *Pres* . . . . . . . . . . . .5J 7
Ringwood Rd. *Pres* . . . . . . . . .2C 8
Ripon St. *Pres* . . . . . . . . . . . . .2H 7
Ripon Ter. *Pres* . . . . . . . . . . . .3F 9
River Heights. *Los H* . . . . . . .5C 12
River Pde. *Pres* . . . . . . . . . . . .6H 7
Riversedge Rd. *Ley* . . . . . . . . .6E 14
Riverside. *Bam B* . . . . . . . . . .6E 12
Riverside. *Pres* . . . . . . . . . . . . .7J 7
(in two parts)
Riverside Av. *Far M* . . . . . . . .2G 15
Riverside Clo. *Far M* . . . . . . . .2G 15
Riverside Ter. *Far M* . . . . . . . .2G 15
River St. *Pres* . . . . . . . . . . . . .5J 7
Riversway. *Ash R* . . . . . . . . . . .4A 6
Riversway Bus. Village.
Ash R . . . . . . . . . . . . . . . . .4E 6
Riversway Enterprise Workshops.
Ash R . . . . . . . . . . . . . . . . .4C 6
Riversway Managed Workshops.
Ash R . . . . . . . . . . . . . . . . .4D 6
Riversway Motor Pk. *Ash R* . . . .4C 6
River Way Clo. *Los H* . . . . . . .5D 12
Rivington Rd. *Chor* . . . . . . . .6J 21
Roberts Ct. *Ley* . . . . . . . . . . .6G 15
Roberts St. *Chor* . . . . . . . . . .1G 25
Robin Clo. *Char R* . . . . . . . . . .5B 24
Robin Hey. *Ley* . . . . . . . . . . .5D 14
Robin Ho. *Pres* . . . . . . . . . . . .5D 14
(off Rodney St.)
Robinson St. *Ful* . . . . . . . . . . .1H 7
Robin St. *Pres* . . . . . . . . . . . . .3D 8
Rock Villa Rd. *Whit W* . . . . . . .6G 17
Rodney St. *Pres* . . . . . . . . . . . .4J 7
Roebuck St. *Ash R* . . . . . . . . . .2G 7
Roeburn Hall. *Pres* . . . . . . . . . .4J 7
Roe Hey Dri. *Cop* . . . . . . . . . .6D 24
Roman Rd. *Pres* . . . . . . . . . . . .5B 8
Roman Way. *Rib* . . . . . . . . . . . .5J 5
Roman Way Ind. Est. *Rib* . . . . . .5J 5
Romford Rd. *Pres* . . . . . . . . . . .2C 8
Ronaldsway. *Ley* . . . . . . . . . .6F 15
Ronaldsway. *Pres* . . . . . . . . . . .1C 8
Ronwood Ct. *Ash R* . . . . . . . . .4F 7
Rookery Clo. *Chor* . . . . . . . . .2E 24
Rookery Clo. *Pen* . . . . . . . . . .3K 11
Rookery Dri. *Pen* . . . . . . . . . .3K 11
Rook St. *Pres* . . . . . . . . . . . . . .2B 8
Rookwood. *E'ston* . . . . . . . . .2D 22
Rookwood Av. *Chor* . . . . . . . .5G 21
Roseacre Pl. *Ash R* . . . . . . . . . .3C 6
Rose Av. *Ash R* . . . . . . . . . . . .1G 7
Rosebank. *Lea* . . . . . . . . . . . . .3A 6
Roseberry Av. *Cot* . . . . . . . . . .6C 2
Rose Clo. *Ley* . . . . . . . . . . . .4C 16
Rose Cotts. *Whit W* . . . . . . . . .2H 21
Rosedene Clo. *Cot* . . . . . . . . . .6C 2
Rose Fold. *Pres* . . . . . . . . . . .1H 11
Rose Hill. *Chor* . . . . . . . . . . .3A 20
Rose La. *Pres* . . . . . . . . . . . . . .1C 8
Rose Lea. *Ful* . . . . . . . . . . . . . .5D 4
Rosemary Ct. *Pen* . . . . . . . . .3G 11
Rosemeade Av. *Los H* . . . . . .5B 12
Rose St. *Far* . . . . . . . . . . . . . .3K 15
Rose St. *Pres* . . . . . . . . . . . . . .5A 8
Rose Ter. *Ash R* . . . . . . . . . . . .3F 7
Roseway. *Ash R* . . . . . . . . . . . .3E 6
Rosewood. *Cot* . . . . . . . . . . . .6C 2
Rosewood Av. *High W* . . . . . .2J 13
Rosewood Clo. *Chor* . . . . . . . .2J 25
Rosewood Dri. *High W* . . . . . .2H 13
Roshaw. *Grims* . . . . . . . . . . . .2K 5
Rosklyn Rd. *Chor* . . . . . . . . . .1J 25
Rossall Clo. *Hogh* . . . . . . . . . .1K 13
Rossall Dri. *Ful* . . . . . . . . . . . . .7G 3
Rossall Rd. *Chor* . . . . . . . . . .6J 21
Rossall Rd. *Ful* . . . . . . . . . . . . .7G 3
Rossall St. *Ash R* . . . . . . . . . . .3G 7
Rostrevor Clo. *Ley* . . . . . . . . .5D 14
Rotherwick Av. *Chor* . . . . . . . .1F 25
Rothwell Ct. *Ley* . . . . . . . . . . .4J 15
Rothwell Cres. *Rib* . . . . . . . . . .7F 5

Rothwell Lodge. *Rib* . . . . . . . .7F 5
(off Grange Av.)
Rough Hey Pl. *Ful* . . . . . . . . . .4H 5
Rough Hey Rd. *Grims* . . . . . . .4H 5
Round Acre. *Pen* . . . . . . . . . .4A 12
Round Mdw. *Ley* . . . . . . . . . .5E 14
Roundway Down. *Ful* . . . . . . .3G 3
Round Wood. *Pen* . . . . . . . . . .5F 7
Rowan Av. *Rib* . . . . . . . . . . . .7G 5
Rowan Clo. *Pen* . . . . . . . . . . .2F 11
Rowan Cft. *Clay W* . . . . . . . . .5E 16
Rowangate. *Ful* . . . . . . . . . . . .4C 4
Rowan Gro. *Chor* . . . . . . . . . .4G 21
Rowberrow Clo. *Ful* . . . . . . . . .5D 4
Roworth Clo. *Walt D* . . . . . . .2E 12
Rowton Heath. *Ful* . . . . . . . . .4G 3
Royal Av. *Ful* . . . . . . . . . . . . . .5J 3
Royal Av. *Ley* . . . . . . . . . . . . .7G 15
Royal Dri. *Ful* . . . . . . . . . . . . .1H 7
Royalty Av. *New L* . . . . . . . . .5E 10
Royalty Gdns. *New L* . . . . . . .5D 10
Royalty La. *New L* . . . . . . . . .5D 10
Royal Umpire Touring Pk.
Crost . . . . . . . . . . . . . . . . .4A 18
Royle Rd. *Chor* . . . . . . . . . . .7F 21
Royton Dri. *Whit W* . . . . . . . .2G 21
Rufford Clo. *Chor* . . . . . . . . . .5F 25
Rufus St. *Pres* . . . . . . . . . . . . .2C 8
Rundle Rd. *Ful* . . . . . . . . . . . . .1H 7
Runshaw Hall. *Eux* . . . . . . . . .2H 19
Runshaw Hall La. *Eux* . . . . . . .2J 19
Runshaw La. *Eux* . . . . . . . . . .4C 19
Rushy Hey. *Los H* . . . . . . . . .5A 12
Ruskin Av. *Ley* . . . . . . . . . . .5J 15
Ruskin St. *Pres* . . . . . . . . . . . . .6B 8
Rusland Dri. *Hogh* . . . . . . . . .1K 13
Russell Av. *Ley* . . . . . . . . . . .6A 16
Russell Av. *Pres* . . . . . . . . . . . .3G 9
Russell Sq. *Chor* . . . . . . . . . .6H 21
Russell Sq. W. *Chor* . . . . . . . .6H 21
Rutland Av. *Walt D* . . . . . . . .2D 12
Rutland St. *Pres* . . . . . . . . . . . .4C 8
Ryan Clo. *Ley* . . . . . . . . . . . .5G 15
Rydal Av. *Pen* . . . . . . . . . . . .2G 11
Rydal Av. *Walt D* . . . . . . . . . .4D 12
Rydal Clo. *Ful* . . . . . . . . . . . . .7C 4
Rydal Pl. *Chor* . . . . . . . . . . . .2F 25
Rydal Rd. *Pres* . . . . . . . . . . . . .2D 8
Ryddingwood. *Pen* . . . . . . . . .6F 7
Ryden Av. *Ley* . . . . . . . . . . . .5A 16
Rydinge. *Clay For M* . . . . . . . .3G 15
Ryecroft. *H'pey* . . . . . . . . . . . .7K 17
Ryefield. *H'pey* . . . . . . . . . . . .7K 17
Ryefield Av. *Pen* . . . . . . . . . . .3H 11
Ryelands Cres. *Ash R* . . . . . . . .4C 6
Rye St. *Pres* . . . . . . . . . . . . . . .3A 8
Rylands Rd. *Chor* . . . . . . . . . .1F 25

# S

Sackville St. *Chor* . . . . . . . . . .1J 25
Sagar St. *E'ston* . . . . . . . . . . .2E 22
Sage Ct. *Pen* . . . . . . . . . . . . .3G 11
Sage La. *Pres* . . . . . . . . . . . . . . .1B 8
St Aidan's Pk. *Bam B* . . . . . . .3E 12
St Aidan's Rd. *Bam B* . . . . . . .3E 12
St Albans Pl. *Chor* . . . . . . . . . .3H 25
St Ambrose Ter. *Ley* . . . . . . . .4K 15
St Andrew's Av. *Ash R* . . . . . . .2E 6
St Andrews Clo. *Eux* . . . . . . . .3B 20
St Andrew's Clo. *Ley* . . . . . . . .7J 15
St Andrew's Rd. *Pres* . . . . . . . .2A 8
St Andrews Way. *Ley* . . . . . . .6J 15
St Anne's Rd. *Chor* . . . . . . . . .1J 25
St Anne's Rd. *Ley* . . . . . . . . . .3A 16
St Anne's St. *Pres* . . . . . . . . . . .2A 8
St Anthony's Clo. *Ful* . . . . . . . .7G 3
St Anthony's Cres. *Ful* . . . . . . .7G 3
St Anthony's Dri. *Ful* . . . . . . . .7G 3
St Anthony's Rd. *Pres* . . . . . . . .2A 8
St Austin's Pl. *Pres* . . . . . . . . . .5A 8
St Austin's Rd. *Pres* . . . . . . . . .5A 8
St Barnabas Pl. *Pres* . . . . . . . . .3A 8
St Benet's Clo. *Bam B* . . . . . . .4D 12
St Catherines Clo. *Ley* . . . . . . .4A 16
St Catherine's Dri. *Ful* . . . . . . . .7G 3
St Chad's Rd. *Pres* . . . . . . . . . . .3C 8
St Christine's Av. *Far* . . . . . . . .2A 16
St Christopher's Rd. *Pres* . . . . . .2A 8
St Clares Av. *Pres* . . . . . . . . . . .5A 4
St Clements Av. *Far* . . . . . . . . .3A 16

St Cuthberts Clo. *Ful* . . . . . . . .1H 7
St Cuthberts Rd. *Los H* . . . . . .4A 12
St Cuthbert's Rd. *Pres* . . . . . . . .2A 8
St David's Rd. *Ley* . . . . . . . . . .4A 16
St David's Rd. *Pres* . . . . . . . . . .2A 8
St Francis Clo. *Ful* . . . . . . . . . . .4A 4
St Georges Ct. *Chor* . . . . . . . .1H 25
(off Halliwell St.)
St George's Rd. *Pres* . . . . . . . . .2K 7
St George's Shop. Cen.
Pres . . . . . . . . . . . . . . . . . .5K 7
St Georges St. *Chor* . . . . . . . .1G 25
St Gerrard's Rd. *Los H* . . . . . . .4A 12
St Gregory Rd. *Pres* . . . . . . . . . .2B 8
St Gregory's Pl. *Chor* . . . . . . . .3G 25
St Helen's Rd. *Whit W* . . . . . .5G 17
St Hilda's Clo. *Chor* . . . . . . . . .4G 25
St Hilda's Way. *Chor* . . . . . . . .4G 25
St Ignatius Pl. *Pres* . . . . . . . . . .4A 8
St Ignatius Sq. *Pres* . . . . . . . . . .4A 8
St Ives Cres. *Pres* . . . . . . . . . . .7E 2
St James Clo. *Los H* . . . . . . . .5B 12
St James Ct. *Los H* . . . . . . . . .5B 12
St James Gdns. *Ley* . . . . . . . . .6C 14
St James Lodge. *Ley* . . . . . . . .6D 14
St James' Rd. *Pres* . . . . . . . . . . .2K 7
St James's Pl. *Pres* . . . . . . . . . .1J 25
St James's St. *Chor* . . . . . . . . .1J 25
St John's Clo. *Whit W* . . . . . . .7F 17
St Johns Ct. *Brough* . . . . . . . . .2K 3
St John's Grn. *Ley* . . . . . . . . . .5G 15
St John's Pl. *Pres* . . . . . . . . . . .5A 8
St John's Rd. *Walt D* . . . . . . . . .7D 8
St John's Shop. Cen. *Pres* . . . . .4A 8
(off Lancaster Rd.)
St Joseph's Pl. *Chor* . . . . . . . . .6H 21
St Joseph's Ter. *Pres* . . . . . . . . .3C 8
St Jude's Av. *Far* . . . . . . . . . . .2A 16
St Jude's Av. *Walt D* . . . . . . . .4D 12
St Leonard's Clo. *Ing* . . . . . . . . .1E 6
St Luke's Pl. *Pres* . . . . . . . . . . . .3C 8
St Margarets Clo. *Ing* . . . . . . . .7E 2
St Margarets Rd. *Ley* . . . . . . . .4A 16
St Mark's Pl. E. *Pres* . . . . . . . . .4H 7
St Mark's Pl. W. *Pres* . . . . . . . .4H 7
St Mark's Rd. *Pres* . . . . . . . . . . .4H 7
St Marlowes Av. *Ley* . . . . . . . . .3A 16
St Martin's Rd. *Pres* . . . . . . . . . .2A 8
St Mary's Av. *Walt D* . . . . . . . .4D 12
St Mary's Clo. *Pres* . . . . . . . . . .4C 8
St Mary's Clo. *Walt D* . . . . . . .4D 12
St Mary's Ga. *Eux* . . . . . . . . . . .4B 8
St Mary's Rd. *Bam B* . . . . . . . .4E 12
St Mary's St. *Pres* . . . . . . . . . . . .4B 8
St Mary's St. N. *Pres* . . . . . . . . .4B 8
St Mary's Wlk. *Chor* . . . . . . . . .7G 21
St Michael's Clo. *Chor* . . . . . . .6F 21
St Michael's Rd. *Ley* . . . . . . . .3A 16
St Michael's Rd. *Pres* . . . . . . . . .2A 8
St Oswald's Clo. *Pres* . . . . . . . .2C 8
St Patrick's Pl. *Walt D* . . . . . . .1E 12
St Paul's Av. *Pres* . . . . . . . . . . . .3A 8
St Paul's Clo. *Far M* . . . . . . . . .6K 11
St Paul's Clo. *Wheel* . . . . . . . .7K 17
St Paul's Ct. *Pres* . . . . . . . . . . . .4A 8
St Paul's Rd. *Pres* . . . . . . . . . . . .2A 8
St Pauls Sq. *Pres* . . . . . . . . . . . .4A 8
St Peter's Clo. *Pres* . . . . . . . . . .4K 7
(off St Peter's St.)
St Peter's Sq. *Pres* . . . . . . . . . . .4J 7
St Peter's St. *Chor* . . . . . . . . . .6J 21
St Peter's St. *Pres* . . . . . . . . . . .4K 7
St Philip's Rd. *Pres* . . . . . . . . . . .2A 8
St Saviour's Clo. *Bam B* . . . . . .6F 13
St Stephen's Rd. *Pres* . . . . . . . . .2A 8
St Theresa's Dri. *Ful* . . . . . . . . . .7G 3
St Thomas' Pl. *Pres* . . . . . . . . . .3K 7
St Thomas Rd. *Pres* . . . . . . . . . .2K 7
St Thomas's Rd. *Chor* . . . . . . . .7F 21
St Thomas St. *Pres* . . . . . . . . . . .3K 7
St Vincents Rd. *Ful* . . . . . . . . . . .6J 3
St Walburge Av. *Ash R* . . . . . . .4J 7
St Walburge's Gdns. *Ash R* . . . .4H 7
St Wilfrid St. *Pres* . . . . . . . . . . . .5K 7
Salisbury Av. *Grims* . . . . . . . . .2K 5
Salisbury Rd. *Pres* . . . . . . . . . . .5H 7
Salisbury St. *Chor* . . . . . . . . . .1H 25
Salisbury St. *Pres* . . . . . . . . . . . .3D 8
Salmon St. *Pres* . . . . . . . . . . . . .5C 8
Salter St. *Pres* . . . . . . . . . . . . . .3K 7
Salt Pit La. *Maw* . . . . . . . . . . .4B 22

Salwick Pl. Ash R ...3C 6
Samuel St. Pres ...4D 8
Sanderson La. Hesk ...7C 22
Sanderson Way. Cop ...7D 24
Sandfield St. Ley ...5K 15
Sandgate. Chor ...3H 25
Sandham St. Chor ...7H 21
Sandown Ct. Pres ...5A 8
Sandpiper Cres. Bam B ...3G 13
Sandridge Av. Chor ...1F 25
Sandringham Av. Ley ...5A 16
Sandringham Pk. Dri.
   New L ...5E 10
Sandringham Rd. Chor ...1F 25
Sandringham Rd. E'ston ...1E 22
Sandringham Rd. Walt D ...2D 12
Sandringham Way. Cot ...5C 2
Sandsdale Av. Ful ...6C 4
Sandwick Clo. Ful ...4K 3
Sandybrook Clo. Ful ...6E 4
Sandycroft. Rib ...2F 9
Sandyfields. Cot ...5C 2
Sandyforth La. L Grn ...4E 2
Sandygate La. Brough ...1F 3
Sandy La. Clay W ...3G 17
Sandy La. Ley ...6J 15
Sandy La. Lwr B & Cot ...3B 2
Sandy Pl. Ley ...6J 15
Sarscow La. Ley ...6A 18
Saul St. Pres ...4K 7
Saunders Clo. Hut ...3B 10
Saunder's La. Hut ...4C 10
Saunders M. Chor ...5G 25
Savick Av. Lea ...3B 6
Savick Clo. Bam B ...5F 13
Savick Ct. Ful ...7H 3
Savick Rd. Ful ...7H 3
Savick Way. Ash R & Lea ...1C 6
Saville St. Chor ...3G 25
Savoy St. Pres ...5J 7
Sawley Cres. Rib ...2F 9
Saxon Hey. Ful ...1G 7
Scarlet St. Chor ...1J 25
Scarlett Dri. Hut ...3C 10
Scawfell Rd. Chor ...3F 25
Sceptre Way. Bam B ...7H 13
Schleswig St. Pres ...4A 8
Schleswig Way. Ley ...5E 14
Scholars Grn. Lea ...3A 6
School Fld. Bam B ...1F 17
School Ho. M. Chor ...1J 25
School La. Bam B ...3E 12
School La. Eux ...4B 20
School La. Ley ...4H 15
School La. Los H ...5K 11
School La. M Side ...5C 14
School La. Whit W ...7F 17
School St. Bam B ...3F 13
School St. Far ...4K 15
School St. Pres ...5J 7
Scotforth Rd. Pres ...4C 8
Scott's Wood. Ful ...5H 3
Sedberg St. Ful ...1H 7
Sedgwick St. Pres ...3A 8
Seedlee Rd. Bam B ...7G 13
Seed St. Pres ...4K 7
Sefton Rd. Walt D ...2D 12
Selborne St. Pres ...6A 8
Selby St. Pres ...3H 7
Selkirk Dri. Walt D ...3D 12
Sellers St. Pres ...3C 8
Sephton St. Los H ...5A 12
Sergeant St. Bam B ...5F 13
Seven Acres. Bam B ...1G 17
Sevenoaks. Chor ...4G 25
Seven Stars Rd. Ley ...7F 15
Severn Dri. Walt D ...3D 12
Severn Hill. Ful ...3G 3
Severn Ho. Pres ...4D 8
   (off Cliffe Ct.)
Seymour Ct. Pres ...2H 7
Seymour Rd. Ash R ...1G 7
Seymour St. Chor ...1H 25
Shade La. Chor ...6H 25
Shady La. Bam B & Ley ...1B 16
Shaftesbury Av. New L ...5D 10
Shaftesbury Av. Pres ...6F 7
Shaftesbury Pl. Chor ...7F 21
   (in two parts)
Shakespeare Rd. Pres ...3D 8
Shakespeare Ter. Chor ...5H 21
Shalgrove Fld. Ful ...4G 3

Sharoe Bay Ct. Ful ...5K 3
Sharoe Grn. La. Ful ...4J 3
Sharoe Grn. La. S. Ful ...7A 4
Sharoe Grn. Pk. Ful ...6A 4
Sharoe Mt. Av. Ful ...4K 3
Sharratt's Path. Char R ...4D 24
Shaw Brook Rd. Ley ...1F 19
Shaw Brow. Whit W ...7F 17
Shaw Hill. Whit W ...1F 21
Shaw Hill Dri. Whit W ...1F 21
Shaw Hill Golf & Country Club.
   ...1E 20
Shaw Hill St. Chor ...1G 25
Shaw St. Pres ...3A 8
Sheep Hill La. Clay W ...4D 16
   (in two parts)
Sheep Hill La. New L ...6D 10
Sheffield Dri. Lea ...2B 6
Sheldon Ct. Pres ...3K 7
   (off Thorpe Clo.)
Shelley Dri. E'ston ...3F 23
Shelley M. Ash R ...3G 7
Shelley Rd. Ash R ...2G 7
Shelley St. Pres ...5A 8
Shepherds Way. Chor ...7H 21
Sheraton Pk. Ing ...5E 2
Sherborne Lodge. Rib ...7F 5
   (off Grange Av.)
Sherbourne Cres. Pres ...1B 8
Sherbourne St. Chor ...1H 25
Sherburn Rd. Pen ...2J 11
Sherdley Rd. Los H ...6B 12
Sherwood Pl. Chor ...7H 21
Sherwood Way. Ful ...5A 4
Shire Bank Cres. Ful ...6J 3
Shop La. High W ...1H 13
Shuttle St. Pres ...4B 8
Shuttleworth Rd. Pres ...2K 7
Shuttling Fields La. Bam B ...4G 13
   (in two parts)
Sibbering Brow. Char R ...7A 20
Sidgreaves La. Lea T ...6A 2
Silsden Av. Rib ...6D 4
Silverdale Clo. Ley ...1K 19
Silverdale Dri. Rib ...6D 4
Silverdale Rd. Chor ...1J 25
Silvester Rd. Chor ...2G 25
Simmons Av. Walt D ...2B 12
Simpson St. Pres ...4K 7
Singleton Clo. Ful ...4K 3
Singleton Row. Pres ...3K 7
Singleton Way. Ful ...4K 3
Sion Clo. Rib ...7F 5
Sion La. Rib ...7F 5
Sir Tom Finney Way.
   Ful & Pres ...2B 8
Six Acre La. Longt ...7A 10
Sizehouse St. Pres ...4K 7
Sizer St. Pres ...3K 7
Skeffington Rd. Pres ...2B 8
Skip La. Hut ...2A 10
Skipton Clo. Bam B ...3F 13
Skipton Cres. Rib ...6E 4
Slade St. Pres ...5J 7
Slaidburn Pl. Rib ...2G 9
Slaidburn Rd. Rib ...2F 9
Slater La. Ley ...6C 14
   (in three parts)
Smalley Cft. Pen ...2K 11
Smith Clo. Grims ...2J 5
Smith Cft. Ley ...6D 14
Smithills Clo. Chor ...6J 21
Smith St. Bam B ...5F 13
Smith St. Chor ...2H 25
Smith St. Whit W ...6G 17
Smithy Brow. Wrigh ...7E 22
Smithy Clo. Brin ...1K 17
Smithy La. Brin ...1K 17
Smithy St. Bam B ...5E 12
Snipewood. E'ston ...2D 22
Snowdrop Clo. Ley ...4C 16
Snow Hill. Pres ...4K 7
Sod Hall La.
   New L & Midg H ...1C 14
Sod Hall Rd. New L ...7E 10
Sollam's Clo. Bam B ...3F 13
Solway Clo. Pen ...2J 11
Somersby Clo. Walt D ...2E 12
Somerset Av. Chor ...6G 21
Somerset Pk. Ful ...4F 3
Somerset Rd. Ley ...4K 15

Somerset Rd. Pres ...3A 8
Sorrel Ct. Pen ...3G 11
South Av. Chor ...2H 25
South Av. New L ...5D 10
Southbrook Rd. Ley ...5H 15
Southdowns Rd. Chor ...2H 25
South Dri. Ful ...4J 3
South End. Pres ...7J 7
Southern Av. Pres ...6C 8
Southern Pde. Pres ...6B 8
Southey Clo. Ful ...4K 3
Southfield Dri. New L ...6D 10
Southgate. Ful ...6H 3
Southgate. Pres ...3K 7
Southgates. Char R ...5B 24
South Gro. Ful ...3J 3
Southlands Av. Los H ...4C 12
Southlands Dri. Ley ...7D 14
S. Meadow La. Pres ...6J 7
S. Meadow St. Pres ...4A 8
Southport Rd. Chor ...6C 20
Southport Rd.
   Crost & Ley ...5A 18
Southport Ter. Chor ...1J 25
S. Ribble Ind. Est. Walt D ...7C 8
South Ribble Mus. &
   Exhibition Cen. ...6J 15
S. Ribble St. Walt D ...6C 8
South Rd. Cop ...7C 24
Southside. Eux ...4A 20
South Vw. Los H ...6A 12
   (School La.)
South Vw. Los H ...6B 12
   (Watkin La.)
S. View Ter. Ley ...6J 15
Spa Rd. Pres ...4H 7
Spa St. Pres ...4H 7
Spendmore. Cop ...6D 24
Spendmore La. Cop ...7B 24
Spey Clo. Ley ...6G 15
Spinners Sq. Bam B ...6E 12
Spinney Brow. Rib ...7D 4
Spinney Clo. New L ...5D 10
Spinney Clo. Whit W ...1F 21
Spinney, The. Chor ...4G 21
Spinney, The. Pen ...2D 10
Spires Gro. Cot ...6C 2
Spring Bank. Pres ...5J 7
Springcroft. Far ...3A 16
Springfield Ind. Est. Pres ...3J 7
   (off Eastham St.)
Springfield Rd. Chor ...7G 21
Springfield Rd. Cop ...7C 24
Springfield Rd. Ley ...7F 15
Springfield Rd. N. Cop ...7C 24
Springfield St. Pres ...3J 7
Spring Gdns. Ley ...6H 15
Spring Gdns. Pen ...3K 11
Spring Mdw. Ley ...5C 16
Spring M. Whit W ...1J 21
Springsands Clo. Ful ...6E 4
Springs Cres. Whit W ...2J 21
Springs Rd. Chor ...5H 21
Spring St. Ley ...5J 15
Springwood Clo. Walt D ...2A 12
Springwood Dri. Chor ...3J 25
Spurrier St. Ley ...2J 15
Square, The. Far ...4K 15
Square, The. Walt D ...7F 9
Squires Clo. Hogh ...3K 13
Squires Ga. Rd. Ash R ...1G 7
Squires Rd. Pen ...6G 7
Squires Wood. Ful ...5D 4
Squirrel Fold. Rib ...2F 9
Squirrel's Chase. Los H ...6A 12
Stackcroft. Clay W ...4E 16
Stafford Rd. Pres ...3A 8
Staining Av. Ash R ...3D 6
Stamford Dri. Whit W ...2G 21
Standish St. Chor ...1H 25
Stanhope St. Pres ...2H 7
Stanifield Clo. Far ...3K 15
Stanifield La.
   Far & Los H ...4K 15
Stanley Av. Far ...4K 15
Stanley Av. Hut ...3B 10
Stanley Av. Pen ...7J 7
Stanley Cft. Wood ...1F 3
Stanleyfield Clo. Pres ...3A 8
Stanleyfield Rd. Pres ...3A 8
Stanley Fold. Los H ...5K 11

Stanley Gro. Pen ...1E 10
Stanley Pl. Chor ...7G 21
Stanley Pl. Pres ...5J 7
Stanley Rd. Far ...2A 16
Stanley Rd. Pres ...1J 25
Stanley St. Ley ...5K 15
Stanley St. Pres ...4B 8
Stanley Ter. Pres ...5J 7
Stanning Clo. Ley ...6G 15
Stansford Ct. Pen ...1H 11
Stansted Rd. Chor ...1E 24
Starkie Ind. Est. Ash R ...2H 7
Starkie St. Ley ...5K 15
Starkie St. Pres ...5K 7
Starrgate Dri. Ash R ...3C 6
Startley Nook. Wstke ...7F 11
Station Brow. Ley ...4K 15
Station Rd. Bam B ...6E 12
   (in two parts)
Station Rd. Cop ...7D 24
Station Rd. Midg H ...3C 14
Station Rd. New L ...5D 10
Staveley Pl. Ash R ...2C 6
Steeley La. Chor ...1H 25
Steeple Vw. Ash R ...4H 7
Stefano Rd. Pres ...4C 8
Stephenage Pk. Pen ...3K 11
Stephendale Av. Bam B ...5H 13
Stephenson St. Chor ...7J 21
Stevenson Av. Far ...3A 16
Stewart St. Pres ...4H 7
Stiles Av. Hut ...4A 10
Stirling Clo. Chor ...1J 25
Stirling Clo. Ley ...5A 16
Stockdale Cres. Bam B ...6F 13
Stocks La. Hesk ...5G 23
Stocks Rd. Ash R ...2G 7
Stocks St. Pres ...4J 7
Stokes Hall Av. Ley ...6J 15
Stonebridge Clo. Los H ...5C 12
Stone Cft. Pen ...3H 11
Stonecroft Rd. Ley ...7F 15
Stonefield. Pen ...1J 11
Stonefold Av. Hut ...4A 10
Stonehouse Grn. Clay W ...3F 17
Stone Pk. Rd. Brough ...1G 3
Stoney Butts. Lea ...4B 6
Stoneygate. Pres ...5A 8
Stoney Holt. Ley ...5C 16
Stoney La. Los H ...7C 12
Stony Bank. Brin ...1K 17
Stonyhurst. Chor ...4G 25
Stour Lodge. Ful ...5G 3
Strand Rd. Pres ...5H 7
Strand St. W. Ash R ...4G 7
Stratfield Pl. Ley ...5K 15
Stratford Dri. Ful ...7H 3
Stratford Rd. Chor ...7H 21
Strathmore Gro. Chor ...1F 25
Strathmore Rd. Ful ...7J 3
Strawberry Fields. Chor ...4G 21
Stricklands La. Pen ...1H 11
Strutt St. Pres ...3B 8
Stryands. Hut ...4A 10
Stuart Clo. Rib ...1E 8
Stuart Rd. Rib ...1E 8
Studfold. Chor ...5F 21
Studholme Av. Pen ...3J 11
Studholme Clo. Pen ...3J 11
Studholme Cres. Pen ...2J 11
Stump La. Chor ...7H 21
Sturminster Clo. Pen ...3J 11
Suffolk Clo. Ley ...1G 19
Suffolk Rd. Pres ...3A 8
Sulby Dri. Rib ...6F 5
Sulby Gro. Rib ...6G 5
Summerfield. Ley ...3H 15
Summerfield Clo. Walt D ...3B 12
Summers Barn. Ful ...5E 4
Summer Trees Av. Lea ...1B 6
Sumner St. Ley ...5J 15
Sumpter Ct. Pen ...3K 11
Sumpter Cft. Pen ...3J 11
Sunbury Av. Pen ...2H 11
Sunningdale. Wood ...1F 3
Sunnybank Clo. Pen ...1J 11
Sunny Brow. Cop ...6E 24
Sunnyhill. Ful ...6C 4
Surgeon's Ct. Pres ...5K 7
Surrey St. Pres ...4C 8
Sussex St. Pres ...3A 8
Sutcliffe St. Chor ...1H 25

Sutton Dri. *Lea* . . . . . . . . . . .4B **6**
Sutton Gro. *Chor* . . . . . . . . .3K **21**
Swallow Av. *Pen* . . . . . . . . . .1J **11**
Swallow Ct. *Clay W* . . . . . .5G **17**
Swallowfold. *Grims* . . . . . . . .2K **5**
Swansea St. *Ash R* . . . . . . . .3G **7**
Swansey La.
   *Clay W & Whit W* . . . . .5G **17**
Swan St. *Pres* . . . . . . . . . . . .4C **8**
Swarbrick Av. *Grims* . . . . . . .2K **5**
Swill Bk. La. *Pres* . . . . . . . . . .6C **8**
Swinside. *Cot* . . . . . . . . . . . . .7B **2**
Sycamore Av. *Eux* . . . . . . . .4B **20**
Sycamore Clo. *Ful* . . . . . . . . .5C **4**
Sycamore Ct. *Chor* . . . . . . . .3F **25**
Sycamore Dri. *Pen* . . . . . . . .2J **11**
Sycamore Ho. *Chor* . . . . . . . .2D **24**
Sycamore Rd. *Chor* . . . . . . . .5H **21**
Sycamore Rd. *Rib* . . . . . . . . . .2E **8**
   (in two parts)
Syd Brook La. *Maw* . . . . . . .7A **18**
Syke Hill. *Pres* . . . . . . . . . . . .5A **8**
Syke St. *Pres* . . . . . . . . . . . . .5A **8**
Sylvancroft. *Ing* . . . . . . . . . . .6E **2**
Sylvan Gro. *Bam B* . . . . . . . .3G **13**
Symonds Rd. *Ful* . . . . . . . . . .1J **7**

## T

Tabley La. *High B* . . . . . . . . .2B **2**
Tag Cft. *Ing* . . . . . . . . . . . . . .6D **2**
Tag Farm Ct. *Ing* . . . . . . . . . .6D **2**
Tag La. *High B & Ing* . . . . . .5D **2**
Talbot Dri. *Eux* . . . . . . . . . . .5B **20**
Talbot Ho. *Chor* . . . . . . . . . . .5G **21**
   (off Lancaster Ct.)
Talbot Rd. *Ley* . . . . . . . . . . . .4G **15**
Talbot Rd. *Pen* . . . . . . . . . . . .7J **7**
Talbot Rd. *Pres* . . . . . . . . . . .5H **7**
Talbot Row. *Eux* . . . . . . . . . .6B **20**
Talbot St. *Chor* . . . . . . . . . . .6J **21**
Talbot St. *Ful* . . . . . . . . . . . . .1H **7**
Tamar Clo. *Ley* . . . . . . . . . . .7K **15**
Tamar St. *Pres* . . . . . . . . . . . .4E **8**
Tanglewood. *Ful* . . . . . . . . . .6B **4**
Tanhouse La. *H'pey* . . . . . . .1K **21**
Tannersmith La. *Maw* . . . . . .3B **22**
Tansley Av. *Chor* . . . . . . . . . .7B **24**
Tanterton Hall Rd. *Ing* . . . . . .5D **2**
Tanyard Clo. *Cop* . . . . . . . . .7B **24**
Tardy Ga. Trad. Cen.
   *Los H* . . . . . . . . . . . . . . .5A **12**
Tarn Clo. *Pen* . . . . . . . . . . . .1D **10**
Tarnhows Clo. *Chor* . . . . . . . .3F **25**
Tatton St. *Chor* . . . . . . . . . . .1H **25**
Taunton St. *Pres* . . . . . . . . . .3D **8**
Taylor St. *Chor* . . . . . . . . . . .3F **25**
Taylor St. *Pres* . . . . . . . . . . . .6H **7**
Tay St. *Pres* . . . . . . . . . . . . . .6H **7**
Teal Clo. *Ley* . . . . . . . . . . . . .7F **15**
Tees St. *Pres* . . . . . . . . . . . . .2C **8**
Teil Grn. *Ful* . . . . . . . . . . . . . .5E **4**
Temperance St. *Chor* . . . . . .7J **21**
Temple St. *Pres* . . . . . . . . . . .5K **7**
   (off Cannon St.)
Temple Way. *Chor* . . . . . . . .3G **21**
Tenby Rd. *Pres* . . . . . . . . . . . .6A **8**
Tennyson Av. *Chor* . . . . . . . .2G **25**
Tennyson Pl. *Walt D* . . . . . . .3D **12**
Tennyson Rd. *Pres* . . . . . . . . .3D **8**
   (in three parts)
Tenterfield St. *Pres* . . . . . . . . .4K **7**
Terrace St. *Pres* . . . . . . . . . . .3C **8**
Teven St. *Bam B* . . . . . . . . . .4E **12**
Thames Ho. *Pres* . . . . . . . . . .4D **8**
   (off Cliffe Ct.)
Theatre St. *Pres* . . . . . . . . . . .5K **7**
Thirlmere Rd. *Chor* . . . . . . . .2E **24**
Thirlmere Rd. *Pres* . . . . . . . . .3F **9**
Thistle Clo. *Chor* . . . . . . . . . .7J **21**
Thistlecroft. *Ing* . . . . . . . . . . .6E **2**
Thistleton Rd. *Ash R* . . . . . . .3C **6**
Thomas St. *Pres* . . . . . . . . . . .5C **8**
Thompson St. *Pres* . . . . . . . . .2D **8**
Thornfield Av. *Rib* . . . . . . . . . .1F **9**
Thorngate. *Pen* . . . . . . . . . . .1F **11**
Thorngate Clo. *Pen* . . . . . . . .1F **11**
Thornhill Rd. *Chor* . . . . . . . . .5H **21**
Thornhill Rd. *Ley* . . . . . . . . . .6F **15**
Thornley Pl. *Rib* . . . . . . . . . . .1G **9**
Thornley Rd. *Rib* . . . . . . . . . .1G **9**

Thornpark Dri. *Lea* . . . . . . . . .4B **6**
Thorn St. *Pres* . . . . . . . . . . . .2C **8**
Thornthwaite Rd. *Cot* . . . . . . .7B **2**
Thornton Av. *Ful* . . . . . . . . . . .7F **3**
Thornton Dri. *Far M* . . . . . . .2G **15**
Thornton Dri. *Hogh* . . . . . . . .2K **13**
Thorntrees Av. *Lea* . . . . . . . . .3B **6**
Thorpe Clo. *Pres* . . . . . . . . . .3K **7**
Threefields. *Ing* . . . . . . . . . . .6E **2**
Three Nooks. *Bam B* . . . . . . .1G **17**
Threlfall. *Chor* . . . . . . . . . . . .5D **20**
Threlfall St. *Ash R* . . . . . . . . .3G **7**
Thropps La. *Longt* . . . . . . . . .6A **10**
Thropps La. W. *Longt* . . . . . . .5A **10**
   (in two parts)
Thurnham Rd. *Ash R* . . . . . . .4C **6**
Thurston Rd. *Ley* . . . . . . . . . .5J **15**
Tiber St. *Pres* . . . . . . . . . . . . .5B **8**
Tiger, The. *Ley* . . . . . . . . . . . .4F **15**
   (off Longmeanygate)
Timber Brook. *Chor* . . . . . . . .5E **20**
Tincklers La.
   *Maw & E'ston* . . . . . . .3B **22**
Tinkerfield. *Ful* . . . . . . . . . . . .4J **3**
Tinkler's Rd. *Chor* . . . . . . . . .2K **25**
Tinniswood. *Ash R* . . . . . . . . .3F **7**
Tintern Av. *Chor* . . . . . . . . . .3H **25**
Titan Way. *Ley* . . . . . . . . . . . .4E **14**
Tithe Barn La. *Ley & Eux* . . .2H **19**
Tithe Barn St. *Pres* . . . . . . . . .4A **8**
   (in three parts)
Tiverton Clo. *Ful* . . . . . . . . . . .3K **3**
Todd La. N. *Los H* . . . . . . . . .2C **12**
Todd La. S. *Los H* . . . . . . . . .5C **12**
Tolsey Dri. *Hut* . . . . . . . . . . .3B **10**
Tom Benson Way. *Ash R* . . . .1D **6**
Tomlinson Rd. *Ash R* . . . . . . .2G **7**
Tomlinson Rd. *Ley* . . . . . . . . .4H **15**
Tootell St. *Chor* . . . . . . . . . . .2F **25**
Top Acre. *Hut* . . . . . . . . . . . . .4A **10**
Top o' th' La. *Brin* . . . . . . . . .3J **17**
Top Rd. *Pen* . . . . . . . . . . . . . .2E **10**
Tormore Clo. *H'pey* . . . . . . . .5K **21**
Tourist Info. Cen. . . . . . . . . . .5J **23**
   (Charnock Richard Services)
Tourist Info. Cen. . . . . . . . . . . .5A **8**
   (Preston)
Tower Grn. *Ful* . . . . . . . . . . . .4K **3**
Tower La. *Ful* . . . . . . . . . . . . .4K **3**
Tower Vw. *Pen* . . . . . . . . . . . .5G **7**
Town Brook Ho. *Pres* . . . . . . .3J **7**
Town Brow. *Ley* . . . . . . . . . .4D **16**
Towngate. *E'ston* . . . . . . . . .7D **18**
Towngate. *Ley* . . . . . . . . . . . .6J **15**
Towngate Ct. *E'ston* . . . . . . .1D **22**
Town La. *Char R* . . . . . . . . . .7K **23**
Town La. *Hesk* . . . . . . . . . . . .7E **22**
Town La.
   *Whit W & H'pey* . . . . . .7G **17**
Townlea Clo. *Pen* . . . . . . . . .2E **10**
Townley La. *Pen* . . . . . . . . . .1A **10**
Townley St. *Chor* . . . . . . . . . .1H **25**
Townsway. *Los H* . . . . . . . . .5C **12**
Trafalgar Clo. *Ash R* . . . . . . .1H **7**
Trafalgar St. *Chor* . . . . . . . . .6H **21**
Trafford St. *Pres* . . . . . . . . . . .2H **7**
Tramway La. *Bam B* . . . . . . .7H **13**
   (in two parts)
Travers Lodge. *Rib* . . . . . . . . .7F **5**
   (off Grange Av.)
Travers Pl. *Ash R* . . . . . . . . . .4G **7**
Travers St. *Ash R* . . . . . . . . . .4G **7**
Trawden Cres. *Rib* . . . . . . . . .7E **4**
Triangle, The. *Ful* . . . . . . . . . .7J **3**
Trigge Ho. *Chor* . . . . . . . . . . .4H **21**
   (off Lancaster Ct.)
Trinity Fold. *Pres* . . . . . . . . . .4K **7**
Trinity Pl. *Pres* . . . . . . . . . . . .4K **7**
Trinity Rd. *Chor* . . . . . . . . . . .1F **25**
Troon Clo. *Eux* . . . . . . . . . . .3B **20**
Troon Ct. *Pen* . . . . . . . . . . . . .6E **6**
Troutbeck Pl. *Rib* . . . . . . . . . .6E **4**
Troutbeck Rd. *Chor* . . . . . . . .3F **25**
Trout St. *Pres* . . . . . . . . . . . . .5C **8**
Trower St. *Pres* . . . . . . . . . . . .6B **8**
Truro Pl. *Pres* . . . . . . . . . . . . .3D **8**
Tudor Av. *Lea* . . . . . . . . . . . . .2A **6**
Tudor Av. *Pres* . . . . . . . . . . . .4F **9**
Tudor Cft. *Los H* . . . . . . . . . .6C **12**
Tudor Rd. *Pen* . . . . . . . . . . . .3A **12**

Tuer St. *Ley* . . . . . . . . . . . . . .4H **15**
Tulketh Av. *Ash R* . . . . . . . . . .3F **7**
Tulketh Brow. *Ash R* . . . . . . . .2G **7**
Tulketh Cres. *Ash R* . . . . . . . .3G **7**
Tulketh Rd. *Ash R* . . . . . . . . . .3F **7**
Tunbridge Pl. *Pres* . . . . . . . . .3D **8**
Tunbridge St. *Pres* . . . . . . . . .3D **8**
Tunley Holme. *Bam B* . . . . .1F **17**
Tunnel Av. *Grims* . . . . . . . . . .2K **5**
Turbary, The. *Ful* . . . . . . . . . . .1G **7**
Turks Head Yd. *Pres* . . . . . . . .5A **8**
Turnberry Clo. *Eux* . . . . . . . .3B **20**
Turner Av. *Los H* . . . . . . . . .6A **12**
Turner St. *Pres* . . . . . . . . . . . .3A **8**
Turnfield. *Ing* . . . . . . . . . . . . .5D **2**
Turnpike, The. *Ful* . . . . . . . . . .5H **3**
Turpin Grn. La. *Ley* . . . . . . . .5K **15**
Turton Dri. *Chor* . . . . . . . . . .6J **21**
Tuson Dri. *Ash R* . . . . . . . . . . .4J **7**
Tuson Ho. *Pen* . . . . . . . . . . . .3J **11**
Tustin Ct. *Ash R* . . . . . . . . . . .4G **7**
Tweed St. *Pres* . . . . . . . . . . . .4H **7**
Two Acre La. *Pen* . . . . . . . . .4G **11**
Tyne St. *Bam B* . . . . . . . . . .4F **13**
Tyne St. *Pres* . . . . . . . . . . . . .6H **7**

## U

Ullswater Rd. *Chor* . . . . . . . .2F **25**
Ullswater Rd. *Ful* . . . . . . . . . .7C **4**
Ulnes Walton La. *Ley* . . . . . .3B **18**
Underwood. *Ful* . . . . . . . . . . .1G **7**
Union St. *Chor* . . . . . . . . . . . .7G **21**
Union St. *Pres* . . . . . . . . . . . . .4K **7**
Union St. *Whit W* . . . . . . . . .6G **17**
Uplands Chase. *Ful* . . . . . . . . .5F **3**

## V

Valentines La. *Cot* . . . . . . . . .7C **2**
Valentines Mdw. *Cot* . . . . . . .7C **2**
Vale, The. *Ful* . . . . . . . . . . . . .6K **3**
Vale, The. *Walt D* . . . . . . . . .3B **12**
Valley Rd. *Pen* . . . . . . . . . . . .7G **7**
Valley Vw. *Chor* . . . . . . . . . . .1J **25**
Valley Vw. *Ful* . . . . . . . . . . . . .7A **4**
Valley Vw. *Walt D* . . . . . . . .2A **12**
Varley St. *Pres* . . . . . . . . . . . . .2A **8**
Ventnor Pl. *Ful* . . . . . . . . . . . . .7E **2**
Ventnor Rd. *Chor* . . . . . . . . . .2F **25**
Vernon St. *Pres* . . . . . . . . . . . .3K **7**
Vevey St. *Ley* . . . . . . . . . . . . .5J **15**
Vicarage Clo. *Eux* . . . . . . . . .4B **20**
Vicarage Clo. *Ful* . . . . . . . . . . .7K **3**
Vicarage La. *Ful* . . . . . . . . . . .7K **3**
Vicarage La. *Sam* . . . . . . . . . .3K **9**
   (in two parts)
Vicarage St. *Chor* . . . . . . . . .6H **21**
Vicarsfields Rd. *Ley* . . . . . . . .7J **15**
Victoria Ct. *Brough* . . . . . . . .1G **3**
Victoria Pl. *Ley* . . . . . . . . . . . .1J **7**
Victoria Mans. *Ash R* . . . . . . .4E **6**
Victoria Pde. *Ash R* . . . . . . . .3F **7**
Victoria Pk. Av. *Lea* . . . . . . . .3B **6**
Victoria Pk. Av. *Ley* . . . . . . . .7F **15**
Victoria Pk. Dri. *Lea* . . . . . . . .3B **6**
Victoria Quay. *Ash R* . . . . . . .5E **6**
Victoria Rd. *Ful* . . . . . . . . . . . .1J **7**
Victoria Rd. *Walt D* . . . . . . . .6C **8**
Victoria St. *Chor* . . . . . . . . . .1H **25**
Victoria St. *Los H* . . . . . . . . .5B **12**
Victoria St. *Pres* . . . . . . . . . . .3J **7**
Victoria St. *Wheel* . . . . . . . . .7K **17**
Victoria Ter. *Chor* . . . . . . . . .6H **21**
Victoria Ter. *Ley* . . . . . . . . . . .6J **15**
Victoria Ter. *Los H* . . . . . . . . .5A **12**
   (off Watkin La., in two parts)
Victory Wharf. *Ash R* . . . . . . .4F **7**
View St. *E'ston* . . . . . . . . . . .1E **22**
Village Cft. *Eux* . . . . . . . . . . .4B **20**
Village Dri. *Rib* . . . . . . . . . . . .2F **9**
Village Grn. La. *Ing* . . . . . . . .5D **2**
Villas, The. *Cot* . . . . . . . . . . . .6C **2**
Villiers Ct. *Pres* . . . . . . . . . . . .2H **7**
   (in two parts)
Villiers St. *Pres* . . . . . . . . . . . .2H **7**
   (in three parts)
Vinery, The. *New L* . . . . . . . .5D **10**
Vine St. *Chor* . . . . . . . . . . . . .6G **21**
Vine St. *Pres* . . . . . . . . . . . . . .4H **7**

## W

Waddington Rd. *Rib* . . . . . . . .2G **9**
Wade Brook Rd. *Ley* . . . . . . .1B **18**
Wadham Rd. *Pres* . . . . . . . . . .6B **8**
Waingate. *Grims* . . . . . . . . . . .2J **5**
Waingate Ct. *Grims* . . . . . . . .2J **5**
Waldon St. *Pres* . . . . . . . . . . . .3E **8**
Walgarth Dri. *Chor* . . . . . . . . .1E **24**
Walkdale. *Hut* . . . . . . . . . . . .3B **10**
Walker La. *Ful* . . . . . . . . . . . . .4E **2**
Walker Pl. *Pres* . . . . . . . . . . . .5B **8**
Walker St. *Pres* . . . . . . . . . . . .4K **7**
Walled Garden, The.
   *Whit W* . . . . . . . . . . . . .1F **21**
Wallend Rd. *Ash R* . . . . . . . . .5B **6**
Walletts Rd. *Chor* . . . . . . . . . .2F **25**
Walletts Wood Ct. *Chor* . . . . .3E **24**
Walney Clo. *Lea* . . . . . . . . . . .3A **6**
Walnut Clo. *Pres* . . . . . . . . . . .2F **11**
Walton Av. *Pen* . . . . . . . . . . . .2F **11**
Walton Grn. *Walt D* . . . . . . .1D **12**
Walton-le-Dale. *Bam B* . . . . .6D **12**
Walton's Pde. *Pres* . . . . . . . . . .5J **7**
Walton Summit Ind. Est.
   *Bam B* . . . . . . . . . . . . .6H **13**
Walton Summit Rd.
   *Bam B* . . . . . . . . . . . . .7G **13**
Walton Vw. *Pres* . . . . . . . . . . .4D **8**
Wanstead St. *Pres* . . . . . . . . . .4E **8**
Warbury St. *Pres* . . . . . . . . . . .3E **8**
Warden Hall. . . . . . . . . . . . . . .1H **19**
   (Arts & Craft Cen.)
Wardle Clo. *Whit W* . . . . . . . .1G **21**
Ward's End. *Pres* . . . . . . . . . . .5A **8**
Wards New Row. *Los H* . . . . .6A **12**
Ward St. *Chor* . . . . . . . . . . . . .1J **25**
Ward St. *Los H* . . . . . . . . . . . .6B **12**
Warings, The. *Hesk* . . . . . . . .4F **23**
Warner Rd. *Pres* . . . . . . . . . . .3D **8**
Warren, The. *Ful* . . . . . . . . . . .5E **4**
Warton Pl. *Chor* . . . . . . . . . .7E **20**
Warton St. *Pres* . . . . . . . . . . . .6H **7**
Warwick Clo. *Ful* . . . . . . . . . . .7J **3**
Warwick Ho. *Pres* . . . . . . . . . .6A **8**
Warwick Rd. *E'ston* . . . . . . . .1E **22**
Warwick Rd. *Ley* . . . . . . . . . .7G **15**
Warwick Rd. *Walt D* . . . . . . .1D **12**
Warwick St. *Pres* . . . . . . . . . . .4K **7**
Wasdale Clo. *Ley* . . . . . . . . . .1K **19**
Washington La. *Eux* . . . . . . . .5C **20**
Waterford Clo. *Ful* . . . . . . . . . .6C **4**
Waterford Clo. *Hth C* . . . . . . .7K **25**
Water Head. *Ful* . . . . . . . . . . .1F **7**
Waterhouse Grn. *Whit W* . . . .7F **17**
Watering Pool La. *Los H* . . . .3B **12**
Water La. *Ash R* . . . . . . . . . . . .3G **7**
Waterloo Rd. *Ash R* . . . . . . . .2F **7**
Waterloo St. *Chor* . . . . . . . . .6G **21**
Waterloo Ter. *Ash R* . . . . . . . .3G **7**
Water's Edge. *Ing* . . . . . . . . . .1D **6**
Water St. *Bam B* . . . . . . . . . .3E **12**
Water St. *Brin* . . . . . . . . . . . .1K **17**
Water St. *Chor* . . . . . . . . . . . .7G **21**
Watery La. *Ash R* . . . . . . . . . . .4E **6**
Watery La. *Pres* . . . . . . . . . . . .4D **8**
Watkin La. *Los H* . . . . . . . . . .5A **12**
Watkin Rd. *Clay W* . . . . . . . .6F **17**
Watling St. Rd. *Ful* . . . . . . . . .1J **7**
Watling St. Rd. *Rib* . . . . . . . . .2K **7**
   (off Churchill Rd.)
Waverley Dri. *New L* . . . . . . .6D **10**
Waverley Gdns. *Rib* . . . . . . . .2E **8**
Waverley Rd. *Pres* . . . . . . . . . .3D **8**
Weald, The. *Cot* . . . . . . . . . . .6B **2**
Weavers Brow. *Chor* . . . . . . .2K **25**
Webster St. *Ash R* . . . . . . . . . .3G **7**
Weeton Pl. *Ash R* . . . . . . . . . .3C **6**
Weirden Clo. *Pen* . . . . . . . . . .4G **11**
Welbeck Cres. *Bam B* . . . . . .4E **12**
Weld Av. *Chor* . . . . . . . . . . . .3G **25**
Weldbank La. *Chor* . . . . . . . . .3G **25**
Weldbank St. *Chor* . . . . . . . . .3G **25**
Wellfield Av. *Ley* . . . . . . . . . . .5H **15**
Wellfield Bus. Pk. *Pres* . . . . . .4H **7**
Wellfield Rd. *Los H* . . . . . . . . .6A **12**
Wellfield Rd. *Pres* . . . . . . . . . .4H **7**
Wellington Av. *Ley* . . . . . . . . .6K **15**
Wellington Pl. *Walt D* . . . . . .3D **12**
Wellington Rd. *Ash R* . . . . . . .3F **7**
Wellington St. *Chor* . . . . . . . .6G **21**

Wellington St. *Pres* . . . . . . . . .4H 7
Well Orchard. *Bam B* . . . . . .1F 17
Wells Fold Clo. *Clay W* . . . . .5G 17
Wells St. *Pres* . . . . . . . . . . . .3C 8
Welsby Rd. *Ley* . . . . . . . . . .6F 15
Wembley Av. *Pen* . . . . . . . . .7F 7
Wensley Pl. *Rib* . . . . . . . . . .7D 4
Wentworth Clo. *Pen* . . . . . . .6E 6
Wentworth Dri. *Brough* . . . . .1G 3
Wentworth Dri. *Eux* . . . . . . .3B 20
Wentworth Pl. *Brough* . . . . . .1G 3
Werneth Clo. *Pen* . . . . . . . . .4K 11
Wesley St. *Bam B* . . . . . . . . .5F 13
West Av. *Ing* . . . . . . . . . . . . .5E 2
West Bank. *Chor* . . . . . . . . .7G 21
Westbourne Rd. *Chor* . . . . . .2F 25
Westbrook Cres. *Ing* . . . . . . .7E 2
Westby Pl. *Ash R* . . . . . . . . . .3D 6
West Cliff. *Pres* . . . . . . . . . . .6J 7
W. Cliff Ter. *Pres* . . . . . . . . . .6J 7
(in two parts)
West Cres. *Brough* . . . . . . . . .1G 3
West Dri. *Ley* . . . . . . . . . . .3B 16
West End. *Pen* . . . . . . . . . . .6E 6
Westend Av. *Cop* . . . . . . . . .7B 24
Westerlong. *Lea* . . . . . . . . . . .3B 6
Western Av. *Eux* . . . . . . . . . .7B 16
Western Dri. *Ley* . . . . . . . . . .5F 15
Westfield. *Los H* . . . . . . . . . .5A 12
Westfield Dri. *Hogh* . . . . . . . .4K 13
Westfield Dri. *Ley* . . . . . . . . .5F 15
Westfield Dri. *Rib* . . . . . . . . . .7D 4
Westgate. *Ful* . . . . . . . . . . . .6H 3
Westgate. *Ley* . . . . . . . . . . .6H 15
Westhoughton Rd.
   *Adl & Hth C* . . . . . . . . . .7K 25
Westlands. *Ley* . . . . . . . . . . .7E 14
Westleigh M. *Cot* . . . . . . . . . .7A 2
Westleigh Rd. *Ash R* . . . . . . . .3D 6
West Meadow. *Lea* . . . . . . . . .1C 6
Westminster Pl. *E'ston* . . . . .7C 18
Westminster Pl. *Hut* . . . . . . . .4B 10
Westminster Rd. *Chor* . . . . . . .1G 25
Westmorland Clo. *Ley* . . . . . .7G 15
Westmorland Clo. *Pen* . . . . . .1F 11
Westmorland Ho. *Pres* . . . . . .4K 7
Weston St. *Ash R* . . . . . . . . . .4H 7
West Paddock. *Ley* . . . . . . . .6G 15
West Pk. Av. *Ash R* . . . . . . . . .2C 6
West Pk. La. *Ash R* . . . . . . . . .2E 6
West Rd. *Ful* . . . . . . . . . . . . .1K 7
West Strand. *Pres* . . . . . . . . .4G 7
West St. *Chor* . . . . . . . . . . . .1G 25
West Vw. *Bam B* . . . . . . . . . .6E 12
West Vw. *Pres* . . . . . . . . . . . .2C 8
West Vw. *Wheel* . . . . . . . . . .7K 17
W. View Ter. *Pres* . . . . . . . . . .4G 7
West Way. *Chor* . . . . . . . . . .6D 20
Westway. *Ful* . . . . . . . . . . . . .7A 4
Westway Ct. *Ful* . . . . . . . . . . .7A 4
Westwell Rd. *Chor* . . . . . . . .6H 21
Westwood. *Ley* . . . . . . . . . . .4J 15
Westwood Rd. *Bam B* . . . . . .2G 17
Wetherall St. *Ash R* . . . . . . . . .3H 7
Whalley Rd. *Hesk* . . . . . . . . .4F 23
Whalley St. *Bam B* . . . . . . . . .3F 13
Whalley St. *Chor* . . . . . . . . . .1G 25
Wham Hey. *New L* . . . . . . . .6E 10
Wham La. *New L & Wstke* . . .6E 10
Wharfedale Av. *Rib* . . . . . . . . .6E 4
Wharfedale Rd. *Ley* . . . . . . . .7J 15
Wheatfield. *Ley* . . . . . . . . . . .6C 14
Wheelton La. *Far* . . . . . . . . . .4J 15
Whernside Cres. *Rib* . . . . . . . .6D 4
Whernside Way. *Ley* . . . . . . .5A 16
Whimberry Clo. *Chor* . . . . . . .6J 21
Whinfield Av. *Chor* . . . . . . . .6H 21

Whinfield La. *Ash R* . . . . . . . .4D 6
Whinfield Pl. *Ash R* . . . . . . . .4D 6
Whinnyfield La. *Wood* . . . . . .1A 2
Whinny Rd. *Eux* . . . . . . . . . . .3C 20
Whinsands Clo. *Ful* . . . . . . . . .6D 4
Whins La. *Wheel* . . . . . . . . . .6K 17
Whitby Av. *Ing* . . . . . . . . . . . .6D 2
(in three parts)
Whitby Pl. *Ing* . . . . . . . . . . . .6D 2
Whitebeam Clo. *Pen* . . . . . . . .2F 11
Whitefield Mdw. *Bam B* . . . . .3F 13
Whitefield Rd. *Pen* . . . . . . . . .1E 10
Whitefield Rd. E. *Pen* . . . . . . .1E 10
Whitefield Rd. W. *Pen* . . . . . .1E 10
Whitefriar Clo. *Ing* . . . . . . . . .6E 2
Whitegate Fold. *Char R* . . . . . .5C 24
Whitehead Dri. *Far M* . . . . . . .3G 15
Whiteholme Pl. *Ash R* . . . . . . .3C 6
Whitelens Av. *Lea* . . . . . . . . . .3A 6
White Mdw. *Lea* . . . . . . . . . . .1C 6
Whitendale Dri. *Bam B* . . . . . .5F 13
Whitethorn Clo. *Clay W* . . . . .4E 16
Whitethorn Sq. *Lea* . . . . . . . .3B 6
Whitmore Dri. *Rib* . . . . . . . . .2G 9
Whitmore Gro. *Rib* . . . . . . . . .2G 9
Whitmore Pl. *Rib* . . . . . . . . . .2G 9
Whittam Rd. *Chor* . . . . . . . . .3F 25
Whittendale Hall. *Pres* . . . . . .3K 7
Whittingham La.
   *Brough & Goos* . . . . . . .1H 3
Whittingham La.
   *Haig & Grims* . . . . . . . . .1H 5
Whittle Brow. *Cop* . . . . . . . . .7A 24
Whittle Grn. *Wood* . . . . . . . . .1C 2
Whittle Hill. *Wood* . . . . . . . . .1C 2
Whittle Pk. *Clay W* . . . . . . . . .4F 17
Whitworth Dri. *Chor* . . . . . . . .1C 24
Wholesome La. *New L* . . . . . .7C 10
Wigan La. *Chor & Hth C* . . . . .7H 25
Wigan Rd. *Eux* . . . . . . . . . . .2A 20
Wigan Rd. *Ley & Bam B* . . . . .7A 16
Wignall St. *Pres* . . . . . . . . . . .3C 8
Wigton Av. *Ley* . . . . . . . . . . .7F 15
Wilderswood Clo. *Whit W* . . . .4G 17
Wildman St. *Pres* . . . . . . . . . .1J 7
Wilkinson St. *Los H* . . . . . . . .5B 12
William Henry St. *Pres* . . . . . .4C 8
Williams La. *Ful* . . . . . . . . . . .4C 4
William St. *Chor* . . . . . . . . . .2G 25
William St. *Los H* . . . . . . . . . .5A 12
William Young Clo. *Pres* . . . . .2C 8
Willow Clo. *Hogh* . . . . . . . . . .4K 13
Willow Clo. *Los H* . . . . . . . . . .5A 12
Willow Clo. *Pres* . . . . . . . . . .1E 10
Willow Coppice. *Lea* . . . . . . . .1C 6
Willow Cres. *Ley* . . . . . . . . . .3B 16
Willow Cres. *Rib* . . . . . . . . . . .2D 8
Willow Dri. *Char R* . . . . . . . . .5B 24
Willowfield. *Clay W* . . . . . . . .3G 17
Willow Grn. *Ash R* . . . . . . . . . .4E 6
Willow Rd. *Chor* . . . . . . . . . . .5J 21
Willow Rd. *Ley* . . . . . . . . . . .1B 18
Willows, The. *Cop* . . . . . . . . .7C 24
Willow Tree Av. *Brough* . . . . .1H 3
Willow Tree Cres. *Ley* . . . . . . .5F 15
Willow Way. *New L* . . . . . . . .6D 10
Wilmar Rd. *Ley* . . . . . . . . . . .4A 16
Wilmot Rd. *Rib* . . . . . . . . . . . .1E 8
Wilton Gro. *Pen* . . . . . . . . . .1E 10
Wilton Pl. *Ley* . . . . . . . . . . . .5K 15
Wiltshire M. *Cot* . . . . . . . . . . .6B 2
Winchester Av. *Chor* . . . . . . . .5J 25
Winckley Ct. *Pres* . . . . . . . . . .5K 7
Winckley Gdns. *Pres* . . . . . . . .5K 7
Winckley Rd. *Pres* . . . . . . . . . .6H 7
Winckley Sq. *Pres* . . . . . . . . . .5K 7

Winckley St. *Pres* . . . . . . . . . .5K 7
Windermere Av. *Far* . . . . . . . .3J 15
Windermere Rd. *Chor* . . . . . . .1J 25
Windermere Rd. *Ful* . . . . . . . . .7C 4
Windermere Rd. *Pres* . . . . . . .3G 9
Windflower Dri. *Ley* . . . . . . . .4C 16
Windsor Av. *Ash R* . . . . . . . . .2F 7
Windsor Av. *New L* . . . . . . . .4E 10
Windsor Av. *Pen* . . . . . . . . . .2G 11
Windsor Clo. *Chor* . . . . . . . . .1F 25
Windsor Clo. *Ley* . . . . . . . . . .7F 15
Windsor Dri. *Ful* . . . . . . . . . . .5H 3
Windsor Rd. *Chor* . . . . . . . . .1F 25
Windsor Rd. *Chor & E'ston* . .1E 22
Windsor Rd. *Walt D* . . . . . . . .2D 12
Winery La. *Walt D* . . . . . . . . . .7C 8
Wingates. *Pen* . . . . . . . . . . .2G 11
Winmarleigh Rd. *Ash R* . . . . . .3F 7
Winslow Clo. *Pen* . . . . . . . . . .3J 11
Winsor Av. *Ley* . . . . . . . . . . .6K 15
Winster Clo. *Hogh* . . . . . . . . .1K 13
Winter Hill Clo. *Pres* . . . . . . . .4J 5
Winton Av. *Ful* . . . . . . . . . . . .5K 3
Withington La. *Hesk* . . . . . . . .6G 23
Within Lea. *Bam B* . . . . . . . . .4E 12
Withnell Gro. *Chor* . . . . . . . . .6J 21
Withy Ct. *Ful* . . . . . . . . . . . . .1J 7
Withy Gro. Clo. *Bam B* . . . . . .4F 13
Withy Gro. Cres. *Bam B* . . . . .4F 13
Withy Gro. Rd. *Bam B* . . . . . . .4F 13
Withy Pde. *Ful* . . . . . . . . . . . .7J 3
Withy Trees Av. *Bam B* . . . . . .5F 13
Withy Trees Clo. *Bam B* . . . . .4F 13
Witton St. *Pres* . . . . . . . . . . . .4B 8
Woburn Grn. *Ley* . . . . . . . . . .4K 15
Wolseley Clo. *Ley* . . . . . . . . . .6J 15
Wolseley Pl. *Pres* . . . . . . . . . .5A 8
Wolseley Rd. *Pres* . . . . . . . . . .7J 7
Woodacre Rd. *Rib* . . . . . . . . . .2G 9
Woodale Rd. *Clay W* . . . . . . . .2F 17
Wood Bank. *Pen* . . . . . . . . . .2G 11
Woodchat Ct. *Chor* . . . . . . . .3D 24
Woodcock Clo. *Bam B* . . . . . .3G 13
Woodcock Est. *Los H* . . . . . . .7B 12
Woodcock Fold. *E'ston* . . . . . .1E 22
Woodcock La. *Char R* . . . . . . .4G 23
Woodcock's Ct. *Pres* . . . . . . . .5K 7
Woodcroft Clo. *Pen* . . . . . . . . .3G 11
Wood End. *Pen* . . . . . . . . . . .4G 15
Wood End Av. *Clay W* . . . . . . .3E 16
Woodfall. *Chor* . . . . . . . . . . . .6F 21
Woodfield. *Bam B* . . . . . . . . . .7J 13
Woodfield Rd. *Chor* . . . . . . . . .1G 21
Woodford Copse. *Chor* . . . . . .1D 24
Woodgreen. *Ley* . . . . . . . . . . .4G 15
Woodhart La. *E'ston* . . . . . . . .3E 22
Woodhouse Gro. *Pres* . . . . . . .5J 7
Woodland Grange. *Pen* . . . . . .2H 11
Woodland Gro. *Pen* . . . . . . . . .7F 7
Woodlands Av. *Bam B* . . . . . .3G 13
Woodlands Av. *Pen* . . . . . . . .2H 11
Woodlands Av. *Rib* . . . . . . . . . .2E 8
Woodlands Dri. *Ful* . . . . . . . . .3J 3
Woodlands Dri. *Ley* . . . . . . . . .5H 15
Woodlands Gro. *Grims* . . . . . .2K 5
Woodlands Mdw. *Chor* . . . . . .5G 25
Woodlands, The. *Ash R* . . . . . .3C 6
Wood La. *Hesk* . . . . . . . . . . . .4F 23
Wood La. *Maw* . . . . . . . . . . . .3A 22
Wood Lark Dri. *Chor* . . . . . . .3D 24
Woodlea Rd. *Ley* . . . . . . . . . . .6H 15
Woodman Cote. *Chor* . . . . . . .5F 21
Woodplumpton La. *Brough* . . .1F 3
Woodplumpton Rd.
   *Ful & Ash R* . . . . . . . . . .7F 3
Woodplumpton Rd. *Wood* . . . .2B 2
Woods Grn. *Pres* . . . . . . . . . . .7J 7

Woodside. *Chor & Eux* . . . . . .4A 20
Woodside. *Far* . . . . . . . . . . . .2A 16
Woodside Av. *Clay W* . . . . . . .5F 17
Woodside Av. *Ful* . . . . . . . . . . .7J 3
Woodside Av. *New L* . . . . . . .6D 10
Woodside Av. *Rib* . . . . . . . . . . .1E 8
Woodside Pl. *Chor* . . . . . . . . .4J 25
Woodstock Clo. *Los H* . . . . . . .5C 12
Woodvale. *Ley* . . . . . . . . . . . .6C 14
Woodville Rd. *Chor* . . . . . . . . .7G 21
Woodville Rd. *Hth C* . . . . . . . .7K 25
Woodville Rd. *Pen* . . . . . . . . . .3H 11
Woodville Rd. W. *Pen* . . . . . . .3G 11
Woodville St. *Far* . . . . . . . . . .3K 15
Woodway. *Ful* . . . . . . . . . . . . .7G 3
Wookey Clo. *Ful* . . . . . . . . . . .5D 4
Worcester Av. *Ley* . . . . . . . . .6K 15
Worcester Pl. *Chor* . . . . . . . . .4J 25
Worchester Gdns. *Cot* . . . . . . .6B 2
Worden Clo. *Ley* . . . . . . . . . .7H 15
Worden La. *Ley* . . . . . . . . . . .7J 15
Worden Rd. *Ash R* . . . . . . . . . .1H 7
Wordsworth Pl. *Walt D* . . . . . .3D 12
Wordsworth Ter. *Chor* . . . . . . .5H 21
Worthing Rd. *Ing* . . . . . . . . . .7E 2
Worthy St. *Chor* . . . . . . . . . . .1J 25
Wove Ct. *Pres* . . . . . . . . . . . . .2J 7
Wray Cres. *Ley* . . . . . . . . . . .1B 18
Wren Av. *Pen* . . . . . . . . . . . . .7J 7
Wrennalls La. *E'ston* . . . . . . . .4C 22
Wren St. *Pres* . . . . . . . . . . . . .3B 8
Wrights Fold. *Ley* . . . . . . . . . .6A 16
Wright St. *Chor* . . . . . . . . . . .7J 21
Wychnor. *Ing* . . . . . . . . . . . . .4F 3
Wymundsley. *Chor* . . . . . . . .6D 20
Wyresdale Cres. *Rib* . . . . . . . . .7D 4
Wyresdale Dri. *Ley* . . . . . . . . .7K 15
Wyre St. *Ash R* . . . . . . . . . . . .3G 7

## Y

Yarrow Ga. *Chor* . . . . . . . . . . .2J 25
Yarrow Pl. *Ley* . . . . . . . . . . . .6F 15
Yarrow Rd. *Chor* . . . . . . . . . . .1J 25
Yarrow Rd. *Ley* . . . . . . . . . . .6F 15
Yarrow Valley Way. *Chor* . . . .3D 24
Yarrow Valley Pk. . . . . . . . . . . .6E 24
Yates St. *Chor* . . . . . . . . . . . .2F 25
Yeadon Gro. *Chor* . . . . . . . . .1E 24
Yeovil Ct. *Pres* . . . . . . . . . . . . .3D 8
Yewlands Av. *Bam B* . . . . . . . .4F 13
Yewlands Av. *Ful* . . . . . . . . . . .5J 3
Yewlands Av. *Ley* . . . . . . . . . .5J 15
Yewlands Cres. *Ful* . . . . . . . . . .5J 3
Yewlands Dri. *Ful* . . . . . . . . . . .5J 3
Yewlands Dri. *Ley* . . . . . . . . . .5H 15
Yew Tree Av. *Eux* . . . . . . . . . .3A 20
Yew Tree Av. *Grims* . . . . . . . . .1J 5
Yewtree Clo. *Chor* . . . . . . . . . .5G 25
Yewtree Gro. *Los H* . . . . . . . .6A 12
Yew Tree Rd. *Walt D* . . . . . . . .7D 8
Yew Trees Av. *Rib* . . . . . . . . . .7G 5
York Av. *Ful* . . . . . . . . . . . . . .7J 3
York Clo. *Ley* . . . . . . . . . . . . .7G 15
York Clo. *Walt D* . . . . . . . . . .2D 12
York Ho. *Pres* . . . . . . . . . . . . .5A 8
York St. *Pres* . . . . . . . . . . . . .1H 25
Young Av. *Ley* . . . . . . . . . . . .5A 16

## Z

Zetland St. *Pres* . . . . . . . . . . . .5C 8